GOD THE HOLY SPIRIT

A Presbyterian Primer

GOD THE HOLY SPIRIT

An adaptation of the
original work by Edwin H. Palmer,
The Holy Spirit

Don K. Clements

Metokos Press
Narrows, VA 24124

Published by Metokos Press, an affiliate of Metokos Ministries, a parachurch ministry providing *"Encouragement for Small Churches."* For current information about all releases from Metokos Press, visit our web site at *www.metokospress.com*.

Cover design by Chip Evans, Walker-Atlanta, Atlanta, GA.

Layout and editing by Diane Hitzfeld, Atlanta, GA.

Printed in the United States by Lightning Source, LaVergne, TN.

ISBN 978-0-9742331-1-6

Introduction to the Series

Presbyterian Primers is a series of medium-length books, written in a non-academic style that I hope will be accessible to the many people (but especially "guys") in churches who do not regularly read books about "church stuff."

Since my seminary days, I have frequently complained that, in arenas other than Reformed and Presbyterian circles, one could find many books written in such a manner. But the majority of Reformed and Presbyterian related works were either designed as adult Sunday School textbooks (with the expectation of a certain level of understanding that goes with such readers), or were written by academics with the hope that fellow academics and a few academically minded people would buy enough copies to cover the cost of publication. There has seldom been literature designed more specifically to reach new or previously unread Church members on topics of importance.

The series will include a growing but not fixed number of titles. This is the second volume, following one on Church government released in 2003. Others may include Church history (pointed towards evangelical American Presbyterian denominations), Old Testament biblical theology (entitled *The Covenant of Grace)*, and several others.

Contents

Foreword

For the last 100 years (since "Azusa Street"), and especially since the charismatic explosion of the 60s, Reformed folks have been wary of studying the person and work of the Holy Spirit. In effect, we have consigned the Doctrine of the Holy Spirit to be the sole purview of Pentecostalism! For anyone who knows the history of the Reformation, these current developments are sad and strange since John Calvin was known as "the theologian of the Holy Spirit" (per B.B. Warfield).

Dr. Clements has done a great service to the modern Reformed Church by resurrecting and adapting Edwin Palmer's *The Holy Spirit* for a new generation. I am hopeful that this excellent work will find a wide audience, especially for adult Christian education classes in our churches. The warmth, practicality and maturity of Don Clements' treatment of these subjects are irresistible and gently draw the reader in. While Don is carefully orthodox, he is not afraid to correct errors and abuses (and there are many, when it comes to contemporary pneumatology!)

The whole book is a solid piece of work, but the chapters on "The Holy Spirit and the World" and the "The Baptism and Fullness of the Holy Spirit" are worth the price of the book. But—if you're going to read just one chapter—peruse the segment on "The Holy Spirit and Guidance." At last, some solid, biblical instruction on a much-needed subject! This book fills a much-needed slot on my shelf.

Carl Robbins, Senior Minister
Woodruff Road Presbyterian Church
Greenville, South Carolina
May 2005

Preface

In 1971, while a student at Covenant Theological Seminary in St. Louis, Missouri, I purchased a copy of a book entitled *The Holy Spirit* written by Edwin H. Palmer, who by that time had become the General Editor of the New International Version (NIV) of the Bible. Palmer was a minister in the Christian Reformed Church who served on the faculty of Westminster Theological Seminary in Philadelphia.

The book had initially been published by Baker Book Company in 1958. My copy was a revision published by Presbyterian and Reformed in 1971. The book had clearly been written to a target audience of laity in the Church with a view to help them understand the work of the Holy Spirit in Bible study format. For a seminary student like me who was just beginning to understand there was such a thing as the "Reformed Faith" this book was truly a Godsend. It helped greatly clarify many of the issues of Reformed Theology that I was struggling to learn from a systematic format. Without a doubt, it was the most important book I read in my second year of seminary.

As the years went on, I would turn to this book time and time again for Bible study and sermonic material. The teaching was so clear it was easily adapted. Thus, when I determined to begin producing a series of Presbyterian Primers, I knew a work similar to this was clearly needed. However, in the nearly 50 years since Palmer initially wrote the book, the reading and understanding level of the average church-going public has declined considerably. The content of Palmer's book seemed to me to be more suitable to seminary students and pastors rather than its originally intended audience. Palmer died in 1980 (see the memorial reprinted from the International Bible Society website at the end of this volume for details about his life). When the copyright on this volume was about to expire in 1984, Baker Books returned it to his family. Not knowing they were required to file a copyright renewal, the family took no action, leaving the original book in public domain.

After discussions with his widow, Mrs. Elsie "Peter" Palmer, as well as one of the four sons, we all agreed that an adaptation of this work—not "dumbed down," but rather written in more up-do-date language, would be appropriate at this time. In fact, it was to exactly this type of task that Palmer dedicated the final several decades of his life; he updated the language of the KJV into the NIV.

It is my hope (and sincere prayer) that this work will inspire a new generation of churchgoers and seekers of truth to come to a rich understanding of the clear biblical teaching concerning the Holy Spirit that Palmer's work provided for me.

Acknowledgements

As always, Soli Deo Gloria!

To Mrs. Elsie "Peter" Palmer and her sons for their willingness and encouragement to see this adaptation put the work of Edwin back into access to a new generation.

To the students in the adult Sunday school at New Covenant Presbyterian Church, Virginia Beach, Virginia, who during the 1980-83 church years were first introduced to the "Presbyterian Primers" concept, including the material in this book.

To Diane Hitzfeld, my editor and formatting guru.

To my many friends and colleagues in the ministry who encouraged me to bring this important work back into print.

Narrows, Virginia
June 2005

[9]In those days Jesus came from Nazareth of Galilee and was baptized by John in the Jordan. [10]And when he came up out of the water, immediately he saw the heavens opening and the Spirit descending on him like a dove. [11]And a voice came from heaven, "You are my beloved Son; with you I am well pleased."

Mark 1:9-11

Chapter One
The Third Person of the Trinity

I f asked, could you explain to someone how to understand the Trinity—the fact that we have one God, in one substance, who exists for eternity in three persons? If you can't, don't feel bad, I'm not sure I can fully explain it either.

I'm not sure anyone can explain it satisfactorily in terms that you and I can totally understand—not that many haven't tried in the past. One of the most famous illustrations is the shamrock—the three-leaf clover. The problem is that the three leaves are identical—and that certainly isn't the case in the Trinity. The only similarity between the Trinity and the shamrock is their "three-ness."

Another famous illustration is the possibility that water, ice, and steam can all exist in the same space at the same time. Given correct lab conditions—the correct air pressure, what have you—it is possible to have water, ice and steam co-exist. However, this won't work as an illustration of the Trinity—because in this illustration there is a limited amount of the basic substance. The more steam you have, the less water you have. The more water you have, the less ice you have. However, in the Trinity there is no limit to the divine substance. In fact, God's substance is omnipresent (which means he is everywhere!)

There are many, many philosophical, logical illustrations—but they are so boring, and some even silly—most aren't even worth wasting our time on. There is one interesting theory however, that was first set forth just a few centuries after Jesus' resurrection. It became known as Modalism, but was soon condemned as a heresy. However, you still see it come back from time to time. Here's how it goes.

Modalism teaches that there is only one substance of God—but that substance takes on three different forms of three different persons. Sometimes the substance appears as God the Father, Sometimes the substance appears as God the Son, and sometimes the substance appears as God the Holy Spirit, but the substance can take on the form of only one person at a time.

When you read the first chapter of Mark's gospel, you immediately see that theory is impossible because there we see all three persons of the Trinity functioning at the same time. In verse 9, we see Jesus being baptized. In verse 10, we see the activity of the Holy Spirit (although we don't see him, because you can't see a spirit—all we "see" is the symbolism of a dove). In verse 11, we hear the voice of God speaking from heaven. All three persons were functioning as separate persons at the very same time...so much for Modalism.

So—what does the Bible teach is the best way to understand the Holy Trinity? Well—let's look at the very best definition one can find—from the Westminster Shorter Catechism Question 6. "How many persons are there in the Godhead? There are three persons in the Godhead; the Father, the Son, and the Holy Spirit; and these three are one God, the same in substance, equal in power and glory."

First, let's focus on the concept of each member of the Trinity being a person. What constitutes personhood? Nearly everyone would admit that a person has a mind that can process knowledge, has a will to decide when to act or not to act, has emotions and feelings, and has the ability to communicate with other persons.

So, God the Father is a person. He's not a cow; He's not the sun; He's not the wind, He's not just an idea or theory (all of which are gods of different groups of people). No, he is a person. Admittedly, he is quite different from persons like you and me. As our young children learn in the children's catechism, "God is a Spirit and doesn't have a body like man." You see, having a body is not part of personhood. It is certainly a part of being a human person—but not part of the concept of personhood.

God the Son—Jesus—is also a person. Before Jesus took on human form on the night we now celebrate as Christmas, he didn't have a body. He was part of the eternal Trinity—and was then a Spirit—just as God the Father.

However, ever since the incarnation, ever since Jesus came to earth to take on human form—to become both truly God and truly Man—Jesus has been a person with a human body! And even now—since the resurrection—He still has a body. It is no longer identical to a human body—the Bible calls it a spiritual body—but it's enough like a human body that we'll have no trouble recognizing any other human we may know when we see them in heaven in their spiritual bodies.

What we must work to understand now is that the Holy Spirit is also a person. He has all the characteristics of a person. Let's look at a few verses from the Bible that will help us see that.

In 1 Corinthians 2:10 we see *"...these things God has revealed to us through the Spirit. For the Spirit searches everything, even the depths of God."* The Holy Spirit doesn't have just any ordinary sort of mind—He has a mind capable of searching the deep things of God.

Acts 16:7 reads, *"And when they had come up to Mysia, they attempted to go into Bithynia, but the Spirit of Jesus did not allow them."* The Holy Spirit has the will to both cause things to happen—or not to happen.

Ephesians 4:30 warns, *"And do not grieve the Holy Spirit of God, by whom you were sealed for the day of redemption."* Clearly, the Spirit has emotions and feelings—He can grieve, certainly a deep emotion.

Never forget this important fact. The Holy Spirit is a person. Never speak of the Holy Spirit as an "it." He's not a thing; he's a person! Of course, he is a person without a body—like God the Father—"a Spirit and doesn't have a body like man."

Notice also that Jesus refers to the Spirit as *"he"* and *"him."* Certainly, Jesus knows that the Spirit is a person.

OK, we're making some progress. The Holy Trinity is three persons—Father, Son, and Holy Spirit—but one substance. That substance is the very nature of God, his divinity. Let's go back to the Westminster Shorter Catechism for the best definition of what that nature, that divinity, is like.

Shorter Catechism Question 4: "What is God? God is a Spirit, infinite, eternal, and unchangeable, in his being, wisdom, power, holiness, justice, goodness, and truth."

Notice, in this definition of God, the term *"Spirit"* applies to all three persons. We must never forget that before the first Christmas, Jesus himself was only a Spirit. So, this definition applies to all three persons of the one God. God the Father has these divine attributes; God the Son has these attributes; and God the Holy Spirit has all of these attributes.

Once again, let's look at a few verses from the Bible that describe these divine attributes in connection with the Holy Spirit. Let's start at the beginning—Genesis 1:2. *"The earth was without form and void, and darkness was over the face of the deep. And the Spirit of God was hovering over the face of the waters."* There is the great, all-powerful Holy Spirit—creating the world, the entire universe for that matter.

Psalm 104:30 reads, *"When you send forth your Spirit, they are created, and you renew the face of the ground."* The Spirit's work doesn't stop with creation. He doesn't just help put the earth in place and then walk away. No, he is involved in an ongoing relationship with the creation. We call it Providence. He *"renews"* the face of the ground.

Then, in the New Testament, Luke 1:35, in the middle of the Christmas story, we find a great verse that teaches us that the Spirit's all-powerful divinity includes supernatural activity. *"And the angel answered her, 'The Holy Spirit will come upon you, and the power of the Most High will overshadow you; therefore the child to be born will be called holy—the Son of God.'"* He is not limited by the natural course of things. He brought about what we all know as the Virgin Birth—a true supernatural miracle.

Not only is the Spirit all-powerful, he is also all-knowing. Look again at 1 Corinthians 2, this time verse 11, *"For who knows a person's thoughts except the spirit of that person, which is in him? So also no one comprehends the thoughts of God except the Spirit of God."* The Holy Spirit is just as all-knowing as is God the Father.

One of the great attributes of God is his omnipresence—His ability to be present everywhere. Well, let's look at this verse, which speaks of that attribute in relationship to the Holy Spirit—Psalm 139:7. *"Where shall I go from your Spirit? Or where shall I flee from your presence?"* The Psalmist has no doubt about it at all—there is nowhere to hide. The Spirit is everywhere! All the divine attributes of God the Father are also true of God the Holy Spirit.

Next, we must understand the relationship between the three persons of the Holy Trinity. You see, there is an order, a hierarchy if you will, in the relationship between these three persons. Even though the Triune God has always existed in three persons, there is an *order* in the Godhead. It is not that the relationship is one of the Father giving birth to the Son. God the Son was not "begotten" in the human sense; he has always existed.

The terms Father and Son do not relate to birth—but rather to role relationships. You and I understand the role relationship of God the Father and God the

7

Son. The Father provides for the Son. The Son does what the Father says. Throughout Jesus' existence, you see that same relationship over and over again.

But what is the relationship of the Holy Spirit to the Father and the Son? Well, the best term to use to describe this situation is the verb "to proceed." Again, a couple of helpful Bible verses, both times with Jesus speaking.

John 15:26 says, *"But when the Helper comes, whom I will send to you from the Father, the Spirit of truth, who proceeds from the Father, he will bear witness about me."* See it there? The Spirit *"proceeds"* from the Father. In other words, the Spirit is sent by the Father to do his will.

One more verse, John 16:7. *"Nevertheless, I tell you the truth: it is to your advantage that I go away, for if I do not go away, the Helper will not come to you. But if I go, I will send him to you."* Not only does the Father send the Spirit but God the Son, Jesus, also sends the Spirit. So it is clear there is a hierarchy, isn't it? Father first, Son second, Spirit third. Sounds a lot like my home: Esther first, Shadow the Cocker Spaniel second, Don third. We all understand our role relationships, don't we?

This issue of proceeding from both the Father and from the Son was at one time a "big deal" in the Church. In fact, it was primarily on this issue that what was originally known just as the Catholic Church split into two major parts—the western section to be known as the Roman Catholic Church and the eastern section to be known as the Eastern Orthodox Church.

By isolating and thus downplaying the work of the Holy Spirit in our lives from the work of Jesus, some modern groups have tended to put Jesus' work of redemption into the background, and bring the sanctifying work of the Holy Spirit more to the forefront. This has resulted, in many cases, to the leading of believers to sense an independence from Jesus and the Church and the Bible, and depending more and more on their subjective communion with the Holy Spirit. While in this book we are focusing on the work of the Holy Spirit, we must always remember that he proceeds from (and therefore is in a subservient role relationship with) God the Father and God the Son.

Also, understand that the Holy Spirit has *three* different names. Sometimes he is referred to as *"the Spirit of God"* or *"God's Spirit."* That usage is in reference to his *"proceeding"* from God the Father. He is also known as the *"Spirit of Christ"* or the *"Spirit of Jesus"*—which is in reference to his *"proceeding"* from God the Son. And of course, most frequently, he is referred to as the Holy Spirit or just a capital "S" Spirit—which is his own name. And—remember what we noted earlier—while the three persons of the Trinity have different role relationships—they are still equal in substance. They just do different things.

OK, now to the real question—*so what?* What does all this really mean to you and to me? What difference does it make in my life that the Holy Spirit is fully God, same in substance, equal in power and glory?

This is Chapter One of a book with twelve chapters, and this book is part of a series of books about basic understanding of what Presbyterians believe. What is so important that we need to spend all this time seeking to understand the person and work of the Holy Spirit? One important thing we need to recognize is that there have been so many differences in the understanding of the Holy Spirit, that churches have split many, many times over just this issue.

Nearly a thousand years ago—in the year 1054—there was essentially only one Church in the world. The one we know today as the Roman Catholic Church. But that Church had a big dispute over their understanding of the Holy Spirit—and split into two parts: one western, one eastern. And still, a thousand years later, the Eastern Orthodox Church is separate from the Roman Catholics.

At the beginning of the 20th Century, some people began teaching new ideas about the work of the Holy Spirit—especially concerning the continuance of some of the miraculous gifts of the Spirit. That resulted in a number of splits.

For just one example, originally there was just one denomination in the United States known as the Church of God. Today we have the Church of God, Anderson, Indiana—and the Church of God, Cleveland, Tennessee, the Church of God in Christ, the Church of God, Holiness and the Church of God in North America. And there are many, many other examples, all resulting from differences in understanding the work of the Holy Spirit. Obviously it is important for us to know at least a little about these differences.

But that's not the most important reason you and I need to understand the Holy Spirit. The *most* important reason is this. Where is God the Father right now? That's right—in heaven. Where is God the Son, where is Jesus? Right again—in heaven. So what about us? Who takes care of us and assists us today? Well—where is the Holy Spirit? He is here. He is with us. He is in us. Of the three persons in the Trinity, the Holy Spirit is who relates to us on a daily, moment-by-moment basis.

Sometimes we use phrases like "We have Jesus in our hearts." However, that's not exactly biblically correct, and we probably should be careful about that. Sometimes it can be very confusing to young children. Jesus has a body. He is located in heaven—so he can't be in our hearts. But the good news is that Jesus sent his Spirit to be our Counselor. He is the person of the Trinity who is with us in our hearts.

11

Let's look once again to those two verses in John's gospel we looked at previously, with Jesus speaking about the Holy Spirit—but this time let's look at what he has to say about what he is sending the Holy Spirit to do! *"But when the Helper comes, whom I will send to you from the Father, the Spirit of truth, who proceeds from the Father, he will bear witness about me."* (John 15:26) See, part of the Spirit's work is to tell us about Jesus.

How about John 16:7? *"Nevertheless, I tell you the truth: it is to your advantage that I go away, for if I do not go away, the Helper will not come to you. But if I go, I will send him to you."* Jesus is giving us an advantage—He is sending us the Spirit as our Helper, our Counselor. It is through the Holy Spirit that you and I relate to God today. And we will flesh this out in detail throughout this book.

There is one other issue that is important. Perhaps it is not the most important—but it is one that is badly lacking in many churches today and in the lives of many Christians. That is how we relate to other people.

Let's look at these three different verses from 1 John 3. Verse 1 tells us, *"See what kind of love the Father has given to us, that we should be called children of God; and so we are."* Verse 11 says, *"For this is the message that you have heard from the beginning, that we should love one another."* Verse 14 states, *"We know that we have passed out of death into life, because we love the brothers."*

OK, follow the progression here. The Father has given us love, (which comes to us through the grace of Jesus, of course). Love gives us assurance that we are children of God. We are to share our love with our "brothers," which means with others in the Church. And ultimately, it is our love of our brothers that demonstrates that we are indeed Christians.

So—think about it this way. If the Holy Spirit is responsible to guide us, to counsel us in our Christian life, what can we say about those Christians who have trouble loving their fellow Christians (which is *all* of us from time to time)? We can't blame the Holy Spirit, can we? Perhaps you are beginning to see just how important the topic of this book really is.

The Holy Spirit is God. He is the third person in the Holy Trinity. He is the same substance as God the Father and as God the Son, whom we call Jesus. God is in heaven. Jesus is in heaven. It is the Holy Spirit who is in us.

As we learn more of the Holy Spirit, my prayer is that you may not only increase your knowledge of the person and work of the Holy Spirit greatly—but that his ministry in your lives will increase even more greatly.

¹Now concerning the coming of our Lord Jesus Christ and our being gathered together to him, we ask you, brothers, ²not to be quickly shaken in mind or alarmed, either by a spirit or a spoken word, or a letter seeming to be from us, to the effect that the day of the Lord has come. ³Let no one deceive you in any way. For that day will not come, unless the rebellion comes first, and the man of lawlessness is revealed, the son of destruction, ⁴who opposes and exalts himself against every so-called god or object of worship, so that he takes his seat in the temple of God, proclaiming himself to be God. ⁵Do you not remember that when I was still with you I told you these things? ⁶And you know what is restraining him now so that he may be revealed in his time. ⁷For the mystery of lawlessness is already at work. Only he who now restrains it will do so until he is out of the way.

2 Thessalonians 2:1-7

Chapter Two
The Holy Spirit and the World

I n the first chapter, we stressed the need for people to better understand the person and work of the Holy Spirit. Not paying enough attention to the Holy Spirit has been a problem in many churches. However, there is an opposite problem in some other groups. They focus way too much attention to just part of the work of the Holy Spirit. They study and discuss and teach almost exclusively the work of the Spirit to get people saved and then how the Spirit supplies them with special gifts.

Now, we will eventually get to this area of the work of the Holy Spirit, but it is crucial to study *all* aspects of this topic. In this chapter, we want to look at his first work—the work of the Holy Spirit in the world. It is best to look at the work of the Holy Spirit in the world in three divisions—creation, re-creation, and common grace. Let's begin with creation.

Most people just naturally assume that when the Bible says that God created the world that it means that God the Father—the first person of the Trinity—is the one who performed this work. They don't realize that God the Son, Jesus, was involved, as was God the Holy Spirit. Creation was the work of the Trinity!

A few Bible verses will be very helpful at this point. *"Then God said, 'Let us make man in our image, after our likeness.'"* (Genesis 1:26) Did you notice that plural pronoun there—*"Let us"*? There is the Trinity; there were three persons involved in creation.

Genesis 1:1-2 reads, *"In the beginning, God created the heavens and the earth. ²The earth was without form and void, and darkness was over the face of the deep. And the Spirit of God was hovering over the face of the waters."* There's the Father—and there's the Holy Spirit.

Now, while Jesus is not specifically mentioned in the Old Testament accounts of creation (since he had not yet taken on human form and the human name Jesus), we are informed of his involvement in the New Testament. Hebrews 1:1-2 tells us, *"Long ago, at many times and in many ways, God spoke to our fathers by the prophets, ²but in these last days he has spoken to us by his Son, whom he appointed the heir of all things, through whom also he created the world."*

OK. The entire Trinity was involved in creation. But the Holy Spirit had several aspects of creation that were left especially to him. One was to embellish, to fill up, the heavens. Let's look at Psalm 33:6. *"By the word of the Lord the heavens were made, and by the breath of his mouth all their host."* There is the Spirit—the *"breath"* creating all the host of heaven.

But the Spirit's greatest creation came on the sixth day. We saw earlier in Genesis 1:26 that the Spirit was part of creating man. But the story gets better. Notice the words of Job. He understood what happened. *"The Spirit of God has made me, and the breath of the Almighty gives me life"* (Job 33:4). Job amplified the act of creation even more. *"But it is the spirit in man, the breath of the Almighty, that makes him understand"* (Job 32:8). The Spirit did not simply create man—but gave him one of the key elements of personhood—a mind, the ability to understand. Certainly, the Holy Spirit was deeply involved in the creation of the world.

He was also centrally involved in the re-creation of the world. We find a good summary of that in 2 Corinthians 5:17, *"Therefore, if anyone is in Christ, he is a new creation. The old has passed away; behold, the new has come."* Today we usually refer to this as being born again or simply "getting saved." But in a very real sense, calling it a "new creation" is appropriate. Actually, this *re-creation* part of the work of the Holy Spirit is so important that we will devote a full chapter to this specific area.

Next, we want to look at the third division of the work of the Spirit in the world usually referred to as common grace. Actually, that is a good title, but it takes a little understanding. You see, all human beings have a problem. It goes all the way back to the third chapter of the first book of the Bible—to Genesis 3. That's where sin entered the world when Adam and Eve disobeyed God and ate the forbidden fruit. Since the Holy Spirit was *not* involved in this horrible act, resulting in the total depravity of the human race, we won't spend time looking at Genesis 3.

What we *do* need to understand today are the effects of that original sin—to be sure we see the enormity of the problem everyone faces. Basically, it amounts to this. A "natural man" (that is a man who has not received the new creation, the new life)—a natural man does not know either God or truth. Pay attention to the following verses carefully.

Romans 1:18 says, *"For the wrath of God is revealed from heaven against all ungodliness and unrighteousness of men, who by their unrighteousness suppress the truth."* The ungodly, the unrighteous *"suppress"* or hold down the truth. In other words, truth does not affect the way they act. Truth would result in godliness, and they want no part of truth.

In 1 Corinthians 2:14 we read, *"The natural person does not accept the things of the Spirit of God, for they are folly to him, and he is not able to understand them because they are spiritually discerned."* Not only does the natural man not accept the work of the Holy Spirit, he can't even understand it.

But this problem is not just a case of making bad choices or not understanding the work of the Holy Spirit, the problem is much, much deeper. Let's look at a few more passages of Scripture.

"The Lord saw that the wickedness of man was great in the earth, and that every intention of the thoughts of his heart was only evil continually" (Genesis 6:5). "...The intention of man's heart is evil from his youth" (Genesis 8:21). The evil is not something learned later in life from the culture—the evil is there at the beginning.

Jeremiah 17:9 laments, "The heart is deceitful above all things, and desperately sick; who can understand it?" Are you starting to see the seriousness of the problem? No one is exempt from this problem. All human beings are in the same boat.

Look at what the Apostle Paul says, speaking in Romans 3:10-12, "As it is written: 'None is righteous, no, not one; [11]no one understands; no one seeks for God. [12]All have turned aside; together they have become worthless; no one does good, not even one.' "

"No one does good, not even one." Actually, this problem is so bad that Paul goes on in Ephesians 2:1 to say, "You were dead in [your] trespasses and sins." That's it in a nutshell, folks. The basic human problem is that every man, woman, boy or girl ever born is dead—spiritually speaking. They have no ability to understand truth or obey God even if they think for a moment they want to (which, of course, they never do).

Now, let me be quick to explain something here. Not every person is as bad as he or she could be. Not everyone is as evil as Hitler, or Stalin, or Saddam

Hussein, or Osama Bin Laden. In fact, some people look pretty good on the outside. Once, in a church I was serving, a lady was trying to describe to me a woman she had invited to be a speaker at a women's ministry meeting. After giving me a glowing description of the speaker and all she had done, she concluded, "I could never be good enough to be a Mormon like she is; I'm just barely good enough to be a Presbyterian."

Laugh if you will—but this is serious. This lady—like far too many church members today—failed to understand this crucial issue. It is never what you see on the outside. It is never what you see that may look like goodness. The issue is that every person—even this wonderful Mormon speaker—without the Holy Spirit coming into his or her life to bring a new heart and a new life in Christ—every person has only evil in his or her heart, because they are opposed to God's truth.

OK—I think we've described the problem thoroughly enough. Let's start thinking about solutions. We have to start by examining several very common erroneous solutions. Some people try to deny the very existence of original sin in human beings. It is a basic premise of humanism today that all babies are born totally innocent and, as they grow up and are influenced by their environment and culture, they learn to do bad things.

Of course, say these humanists, the children who grow up in the worst environments and culture—in poor, urban areas—learn the worst things. This theory has been around for decades. It even resulted in Leonard Bernstein writing a famous line for a gang character in West Side Story, who explains to one officer Krupski, "I'm depraved because I'm deprived." Well, the gang member was wrong. He was depraved because he was born that way. He was totally depraved, as a result of original sin. This erroneous humanist solution denies all the teaching of the word of God.

The other erroneous solution goes to the other extreme. It acknowledges that all men are evil and deserve punishment—but says that since God is love, he would never punish any of his creation; therefore, everyone goes to heaven. "Pick your god or your religion—it doesn't matter. Everyone ends up OK."

But what does Jesus have to say about this error? I'm sure you know the verse, John 3:16. *"For God so loved the world, that he gave his only Son, that whoever believes in him should not perish but have eternal life."* It's pretty clear when Jesus says it, isn't it? You have two choices—believe in him or perish in hell. So—we've still got our problem, don't we? Just what, then, is the correct solution, the only solution, the only way to heaven? Well—it is the work of the Holy Spirit to bring about our new creation, our new life, which, as we said earlier, will be the heart of this book.

You may not see this, but there is yet one more question that needs to be answered. Many people don't think about this very often, but it is important. We know there are people who are not going to heaven, and we know that they have only evil in their hearts—just as we once did. What happens to them?

Well — obviously, the long-term picture is not pretty. But in this life, it is not as bad as it could be. Lots of people are pretty nice. Many of them even do very good things. Why is that? How does that happen? Well, this also is the work of the Holy Spirit. This is the third division of the Spirit's work in the world—the division we call common grace.

We understand saving grace—the work of the Spirit to save us, right? Well, the work he does with the rest of the world is different from saving grace. And so writers have for many years called it common grace (because it is common to all mankind, whether they are God's elect or not. We all have the blessings of this type of God's grace in common). Not all these people are saved; but the Spirit does a work of grace in their lives anyway. Just as Jesus himself said, *"The rain falls on the just and the unjust."* (Matthew 5:45)

You see, it is the work of the Holy Spirit to restrain evil in the lives of people. The best biblical example of this is the story of Noah and the ark. We usually stress what happened to Noah and his family, but we forget what happened to everyone else on earth. The purpose of the flood was to restrain evil on the earth—it was so bad, God couldn't stand any more. He brought the great flood to destroy all human beings on the earth other than Noah and his family.

That was a supernatural act of God to restrain evil. Sometimes he works through a natural act. Many immoral people die directly as a result of their immorality, especially those involved with drugs or promiscuous sex.

Can you even imagine what the world would be like if the Holy Spirit was not at work restraining sin? Can you imagine a world in which everyone was as evil as he or she could be? Whuuuuh—that is scary!

That is the focus of 2 Thessalonians 2. Paul gives a picture of how bad things can be in that passage ... rebellion, lawlessness, destruction, opposing God. But notice what Paul reminds us about in verse 7. *"For the mystery of lawlessness is already at work. Only he who now restrains it will do so until he is out of the way."* Did you see it there? *"Only he who now restrains"* the lawlessness, the Holy Spirit will keep doing his work right to the end.

And the primary way he does that is through common grace. To those we call the natural man—a biblical euphemism for non-Christians, the Spirit provides gifts and abilities that some can and do use for the common good. It's not the same "good" that a Christian performs as "good works" because true good works are all done to glorify God. The natural man has no concept of glorifying God—he thinks he is doing it for himself, or if he thinks he is altruistic, he does it for "others." But it is a different kind of "good works" than that which Christians produce.

One of the best illustrations of this kind of common grace comes from civic activity. Like every locality in the nation, your city or county has its own United Way. People, usually at work, give annual donations so that many of the non-profit organizations in that area can exist. The government also carries out common grace through welfare and Medicaid. There was a time the churches in the United States did this work through their mercy ministries—but now it has been left in the hands of the government or NGO's (Non-Governmental Organizations). Either way, it is the Holy Spirit working through secular means to carry out common grace.

I was once involved in a project that was very much an illustration of common grace through my local Rotary Club. We started a project that raised $8,000 with which we bought and set up eight state-of-the-art computers with all the software in a nice, air-conditioned computer-training center—in the heart of a poor, rural village in the sugar cane fields of Belize!

But remember—it doesn't matter how far-reaching God's common grace might be or how many of these good deeds someone may do—it can never save them. Paul's famous statement in Ephesians 2:8-9 stresses that, *"For by grace you have been saved through faith. And this is not your own doing; it is the gift of God, [9]not a result of works, so that no one may boast."*

So, the work of the Holy Spirit to restrain sin is what we call common grace. The work of the Holy Spirit to save us is what we call saving grace. We should be sure in our lives that we have been saved by the grace of the Holy Spirit—that our personal sin problem has been resolved. If you are not sure, you need to do something about it today, that is, contact a pastor or other mature Christian. Please don't count on your worldly good works to get you to heaven—it'll never happen.

You and I should thank God regularly that he does provide common grace to the lost world—to keep it from becoming as evil as it could. And perhaps you can even find ways to be part of the work of common grace through mercy ministries in your church, because common grace frequently gives us common ground to start a relationship that could result in evangelism taking place. The Holy Spirit, through his saving grace, may move someone who is the recipient of God's common grace to turn his life over to Jesus forever.

¹⁹And we have something more sure, the prophetic word, to which you will do well to pay attention as to a lamp shining in a dark place, until the day dawns and the morning star rises in your hearts, ²⁰knowing this first of all, that no prophecy of Scripture comes from someone's own interpretation. ²¹For no prophecy was ever produced by the will of man, but men spoke from God as they were carried along by the Holy Spirit.

2 Peter 1:19-21

Chapter Three
The Holy Spirit and the Bible

At one point in my college career I was a math major and for some totally unknown (even to me) reason, a philosophy minor! One of the courses I took was Epistemology—which is the study of the nature and theory of knowledge. In other words, how does anyone know anything? After all, a philosopher can't just say he knows something because he knows it—he has to understand why and how he knows it.

Anyway, let me summarize what I learned in that class. At the end of day, all you can really understand is that knowledge and truth are relative. Man keeps trying to know things for sure, wants to know truth—but he can't quite get there. Back in those college days, I wasn't a Christian. Later in life, I learned how to truly know something. In fact, there is only *one* way to find truth—and that is to find it in God's revelation to man. God's word is so very true that one writer refers to it as "true truth" to separate it from the "relative truth" that exists in our world.

How wonderful it is for Christians to know and understand that the great God of creation has revealed his truth to us. And that revelation comes to us in two major ways. One way we call General Revelation. The other we call Special Revelation.

First, let's take a very quick look at the concept of General Revelation.

The Bible tells us that we can know at least something about God just by looking at nature, at the world around us. The author of Psalm 19 puts it this way, *"The heavens declare the glory of God, and the sky above proclaims his handiwork. Day to day pours out speech, and night to night reveals knowledge"* (verses 1-2). In the New Testament, Paul puts it this way in Romans 1:20, *"For his invisible attributes, namely, his eternal power and divine nature, have been clearly perceived, ever since the creation of the world, in the things that have been made. So they are without excuse."* We can't know everything from this general revelation, but we at least know that God exists and that he is all-powerful—and, that left on our own, mankind has no excuse, no hope.

The second major category or way in which God reveals himself and his will is through what is known as Special Revelation. It is appropriate to think of General Revelation as natural and Special Revelation as supernatural.

In Old Testament times, as well as during the life of Jesus, God would reveal himself in supernatural ways on a regular basis. These were "theophanies"— the actual presence of God in some earthly form, such as the burning bush that spoke to Moses and the pillar of smoke that guided the children of Israel through the wilderness.

One special form of these theophanies was the appearance of angels. There were many instances where angels spoke for God, one of whom was in fact a pre-incarnation appearance of Jesus, the second person of the Trinity. We see him dealing with Joshua and the prophet Zechariah, to name just a couple of instances.

There were also many occasions in which God revealed himself through dreams and visions. You may recall Jacob seeing the vision of a ladder to heaven and the Apostle Peter's famous vision of the sheet filled with unclean animals.

A number of times God would actually speak directly to people. God called to the very young boy Samuel in the temple. In the gospels, we hear God speaking to everyone listening during Jesus' baptism and again during Jesus' transfiguration.

Of course, the most important way in which God used supernatural revelation was through his beloved Son, Jesus. Listen to the author of Hebrews, who begins his book with these words, *"Long ago, at many times and in many ways, God spoke to our fathers by the prophets, but in these last days he has spoken to us by his Son, whom he appointed the heir of all things, through whom also he created the world."* (1:1-2)

All of these supernatural forms were important because they gave a clear and certain knowledge as to God's plans and commands. The problem with these forms is that because of the effect of sin, the ability of mankind to transmit the content of this revelation from generation to generation could not be perfect. Even eyewitnesses can be very faulty, as every police detective soon learns. And, since the days of Jesus and the early Church, there are no prophets, no apostles—and most of all, there is no Jesus physically on earth.

So, in his great wisdom, God decided to reveal himself to mankind in a *very* special revelation. Let's start with the classic text on this issue—2 Peter 1:19-21. *"And we have something more sure, the prophetic word, to which you will do well to pay attention as to a lamp shining in a dark place, until the day dawns and the morning star rises in your hearts, [20]knowing this first of all, that no prophecy of Scripture comes from someone's own interpretation. [21]For no prophecy was ever produced by the will of man, but men spoke from God as they were carried along by the Holy Spirit."*

Notice several quick things from this text. One— Peter is referring to the written word of prophecy and is saying that it is more perfect. It doesn't have the problems of oral communication. Remember, in those days, they had in writing the Law and the Prophets, that is, the Old Testament.) Two—it says the word is a lamp, a light to show us the way. We need this written word in order to know what God wants us to think, say, and do. And three—and the heart of this chapter—it was the primary work of the Holy Spirit to make sure the written word (that you and I know as the Bible) was inspired and without error.

Several additional verses will help solidify in your minds this great truth about the work of the Holy Spirit. In Acts 1:16, the Apostle Peter stood up to address all the disciples about the need to replace Judas as one of the Twelve. He refers to the written word this way, *"Brothers, the Scripture had to be fulfilled, which the Holy Spirit spoke beforehand by the mouth of David concerning Judas, who became a guide to those who arrested Jesus."* Peter clearly understood that the Holy Spirit was the agency by which the Old Testament author of Scripture (in this case David) had been able to speak with authority.

The Apostle Paul says this of the words he was writing in one of his letters (1 Corinthians 2:13). *"And we impart this in words not taught by human wisdom but taught by the Spirit, interpreting spiritual truths to those who are spiritual."* Again, we see the Holy Spirit at work—actually teaching and at the same time interpreting the words of the Bible.

So it is absolutely clear that it was the work of the Holy Spirit to inspire the written word of God in the Bible—both Old and New Testaments. But this begs the next question: how did he do it? What method did the Holy Spirit use in this regard?

Before we look at the correct answers to those questions, let's quickly set aside the wrong answers. The Holy Spirit does not do this through nature; through his work of common grace (see Chapter Two). We can know something about God through natural revelation, but that is no help to us to understand what we are to believe or do.

The Holy Spirit did not do it by making a few of God's servants a little more holy than the rest of us. Never believe that the prophets of the Old Testament or apostles of the New Testament were somehow holy enough to write the Bible. No, they were regular sinners, just like you and me.

Furthermore, the Holy Spirit did not simply dictate the words that the authors of the books were to write. There was nothing mechanical about the writing of Scripture. It is true that the authors had a "passive" side to their work in writing the Bible. They did not cooperate in some way with the Holy Spirit, so that the Bible is half from man and half from God. What was written in the Bible was totally at the will of the Holy Spirit—that was made clear in verse 21 of our key text in 2 Peter 1. *"For no prophecy was ever produced by the will of man, but men spoke from God as they were carried along by the Holy Spirit."*

We'll look at this concept of being *"carried along"* in just a moment when we talk about the active side of the author's involvement. But one more verse is key to understanding that this was really the work of the Holy Spirit—a very important verse to learn and to understand—2 Timothy 3:16, *"All Scripture is breathed out by God and profitable for teaching, for reproof, for correction, and for training in righteousness."*

This concept of having been *"breathed out"* is important for each of us to remember when we think about the Bible. While he did not dictate the actual words, the Holy Spirit in a supernatural, miraculous way expired (*"breathed out"*) the truth to the authors who then inspired (breathed in) that truth as they wrote.

As you can see, the authors of Scripture had no part in bringing about the inspiration of the Bible. They were *"carried along,"* and that action was solely the work of the Holy Spirit. Yet they did have an active side to the process.

It's kind of the same way you and I function as individual Christians. Listen to Paul's teaching on this topic in Philippians 2:12-13, *"...work out your own salvation with fear and trembling, [13]for it is God who works in you, both to will and to work for his good pleasure."* Yes, God does work in us to accomplish his goals, but we still have to somehow *"work [it] out,"* even with *"fear and trembling,"* (more on that in the chapter on "The Holy Spirit and Sanctification").

Here's how the authors were *"carried along";* that is, how they actively took part in writing the Bible. First, they were able to maintain their own individuality. David's love for nature appears everywhere in the Psalms. Paul was a great scholar and his acquaintance with all the literature of his day is obvious in his speeches in Acts and in many of his letters. Luke shows the depth of his medical knowledge time after time.

Additionally, the authors of Scripture were not forced to write against their will. There is no evidence anywhere that they were anything but thrilled to be used to put the word of God in writing for the rest of the world. The Holy Spirit ensured that all circumstances in the lives of the authors prepared the way for each of them to be God's man for the job.

The result of all this is that the Bible is a book totally unlike any other. The Bible is the very word of God. You and I can have absolute certainty of the truth (the "true truth," if you will) of the Bible.

But the Holy Spirit did not end his work with the inspiration for the Bible. As great as that work was, it wasn't enough. Because of the effect of sin in the life of every human being in the world, left to ourselves you and I could never understand the Bible. Now, there's nothing wrong with God's revelation in his word. The problem is in our sinful nature—what we spoke of as Total Depravity in Chapter Two. So the Holy Spirit continues to do an additional work in relation to the Bible. This is normally referred to as the work of Illumination.

Before you or I became a Christian, we were not only dead in the trespasses of our sin—we were spiritually blind. We could not see or understand God's truth, (what we have referred to as "true truth.") But when the Holy Spirit comes to regenerate us, he provides his ministry of illumination so we can see the truth in God's word.

In both 1 and 2 Corinthians, Paul talks about this subject in a number of places. Let's look at just a few of those verses. In 1 Corinthians 2:14, Paul writes, *"The natural person does not accept the things of the Spirit of God, for they are folly to him, and he is not able to understand them because they are spiritually discerned."* You see, in order to understand *"the things of the Spirit of God,"* you and I need help; we need spiritual discernment.

Then, in 2 Corinthians, Paul uses an analogy to liken our spiritual blindness to the veil that Moses wore over his face after he had received direct revelation from God. The passage is in chapter 3:12-17. *"Since we have such a hope, we are very bold, [13]not like Moses, who would put a veil over his face so that the Israelites might not gaze at the outcome of what was being brought to an end. [14]But their minds were hardened. For to this day, when they read the old covenant, that same veil remains unlifted, because only through Christ is it taken away. [15]Yes, to this day whenever Moses is read a veil lies over their hearts. [16]But when one turns to the Lord, the veil is removed. [17]Now the Lord is the Spirit, and where the Spirit of the Lord is, there is freedom."*

Do you see what Paul is saying? The veil over Moses face is like the veil over the unbeliever's understanding, particularly their understanding of the Bible. Notice, the veil is not over the word—it is over our hearts, our understanding! But, as he says in verse 16, *"But when one turns to the Lord, the veil is removed."* For a Christian, there is no veil—God has lifted the veil so we can understand his word.

Verse 17 makes it clear—it is the third person of the Trinity, the Holy Spirit, who does the work of lifting the veil. *"Now the Lord is the Spirit, and where the Spirit of the Lord is, there is freedom."* Because of the Holy Spirit's work of illumination, you and I as Christians can comprehend the Bible.

Please understand that the work of the Holy Spirit in illumination is not some new revelation, some special work of grace that comes only to certain Christians. This work of illumination is for *all* believers. I guess the best illustration for this is that of a telescope. When you look through an instrument like that, you still see the very same thing that you can see with a naked eye. But you see it much closer up, much clearer, much better. In fact, what to your eye looks like nothing at all, with the aid of the telescope, you can see clearly. That's what the Holy Spirit does to a believer—all of a sudden, we are able to understand the inspired word of God in the Bible.

You and I as Christians can be very thankful that God has given us his word in the Bible through the Spirit's work. And we can be thankful for the Spirit's work of illumination. But even knowing and being thankful for all of this is not sufficient, because you and I must put all of this wonderful work to use. We must put our eyes on the business end of that telescope and start figuring things out.

And so we need to pray earnestly for the work of the Holy Spirit to illuminate the word of God in such a way that we can understand what we read in the Bible and what we hear in Sunday school lessons and sermons. In such a way that we grow in grace and sanctification daily. In such a way that we can understand the word well enough to share it with others in evangelism.

[1]And Jesus, full of the Holy Spirit, returned from the Jordan and was led by the Spirit in the wilderness [2]for forty days, being tempted by the devil. And he ate nothing during those days. And when they were ended, he was hungry. [3]The devil said to him, "If you are the Son of God, command this stone to become bread." [4]And Jesus answered him, "It is written, 'Man shall not live by bread alone.'" [5]And the devil took him up and showed him all the kingdoms of the world in a moment of time, [6]and said to him, "To you I will give all this authority and their glory, for it has been delivered to me, and I give it to whom I will. [7]If you, then, will worship me, it will all be yours." [8]And Jesus answered him, "It is written, 'You shall worship the Lord your God, and him only shall you serve.'" [9]And he took him to Jerusalem and set him on the pinnacle of the temple and said to him, "If you are the Son of God, throw yourself down from here, [10]for it is written, 'He will command his angels concerning you, to guard you,' [11]and 'On their hands they will bear you up, lest you strike your foot against a stone.'" [12]And Jesus answered him, "It is said, 'You shall not put the Lord your God to the test.'" [13]And when the devil had ended every temptation, he departed from him until an opportune time. [14]And Jesus returned in the power of the Spirit to Galilee, and a report about him went out through all the surrounding country.

Luke 4:1-14

Chapter Four
The Holy Spirit and Jesus

Y ou would agree, wouldn't you, that there are some people who just seem very, very special? Especially well known people like sports stars, great entertainers, well-known politicians, what have you.

I would venture to say that just about anyone reading this book would be awestruck if the President of the United States, or the NFL's most valuable player, or one of the top supermodels of your day were to walk into the room where you are sitting right now! But isn't it also true that once you got to know *any* of these people on a close, personal basis, you would quickly learn of their humanness. You would discover that, after all, other than being really rich and famous, they are not that much different from you and me.

All humans are alike—especially in the one thing we all have in common—original sin. All humans, that is, except for one. Of course, you already know, that I'm talking about Jesus. Jesus was a human like no other. That awe would never wear off as you got to know him better. And yet, the *one* difference between you or me, and Jesus, is that *we* are sinners, and he was sinless. That is the *only* real difference in our humanness.

In this chapter, as we continue our examination of the work of God the Holy Spirit, we want to examine the Spirit's relationship to Jesus. Not just that they are both part of the divine Godhead, the second and third persons of the Trinity. But, rather, that in his human nature, Jesus needed the work of the Holy Spirit. Just like we do!

I'll rather quickly run through a number of areas where that is true, but hopefully you'll begin to see the reality of this point that Jesus needed the work of the Holy Spirit.

To begin with, many people—when thinking about the sinlessness of Jesus—just assume that since he was both God and man, sinlessness was just part of his divine nature. That is not the case. If it were, then he would not have been fully man. Actually, we are told in the Bible that Jesus was subjected to *real* temptation just like you and I face. Look at Hebrews 4:15. *"For we do not have a high priest who is unable to sympathize with our weaknesses, but one who in every respect has been tempted as we are, yet without sin."*

Luke makes a big point in the early verses of chapter 4 of his gospel about the work in Jesus' life of the Holy Spirit in overcoming temptation. He recounts the episode during which Jesus was tempted by Satan himself after spending 40 days in the desert in fasting and prayer. Look at just the first verse of that section, Luke 4:1, *"And Jesus, full of the Holy Spirit, returned from the Jordan and was led by the Spirit in the wilderness."*

And then the last verse, Luke 4:14, *"And Jesus returned in the power of the Spirit to Galilee..."* Luke wants to make it very clear that Jesus needed the power of the Holy Spirit to overcome the temptations of Satan.

Now, ask yourself this question. If Jesus needed the power of the Holy Spirit to overcome sin—how much more do you and I also need the Spirit's power? We are bombarded by temptation every day. Everywhere we go—home, school, work, driving down the street, going to a sporting event or what have you.

Let me give you a personal confession to demonstrate this point. My wife Esther and I are big fans of women's college basketball in general, and most specifically of the Virginia Tech Hokies. We go to just about every one of their home games. During each game, I usually go to the restroom three times. Now, please understand, this confession is not about prostate or bladder problems. This confession is about the fact that I just find it easier not to be tempted when the Hi-Techs dance team takes the floor. I just walk out! Like so many college female dance teams these days, they are dressed in far from modest clothing and perform routines that seem to get more and more vulgar every year.

You and I need to do everything we can to avoid temptation. When it confronts us—and it certainly will, there's no way to avoid it in our culture—then we must be able to stand up to it. To do what we need to do to overcome it. We can't get that power on our own. We desperately need the work of the Holy Spirit to help us in such cases.

OK, let's look at another area of Jesus' life. Consider the simple fact that he had to grow up, he had to mature. The Bible tells us that even Jesus, the Son of God, because he was a human being, had to grow up just like every other human being. Luke tells us in his gospel, chapter 2, verse 40, *"And the child grew and became strong, filled with wisdom..."*

From where do you think his wisdom came? Where did he seek his total spiritual and intellectual growth? Well, that was predicted by the Prophet Isaiah himself. *"There shall come forth a shoot from the stump of Jesse, and a branch from his roots shall bear fruit. And the Spirit of the Lord shall rest upon him, the Spirit of wisdom and understanding, the Spirit of counsel and might, the Spirit of knowledge and the fear of the Lord."* (11:1-2) You see, Jesus needed the work of the Holy Spirit to enable him to grow up, to gain wisdom, and knowledge, and understanding, and might, and even the fear of the Lord.

Again, does this apply to us? Well, we too must grow up. Frankly, that's something we should be doing all our lives, right? The fact is humans don't even reach the stage of being really "grown up" (or substantially mature) until they're about 30 or so. Jesus didn't set out on his ministry until after he had turned 30. I don't know very many young people—especially young men—who appear to be very mature before they reach that age.

And the elements of our growing up, of our maturing, need to come from the work of the Holy Spirit. True wisdom isn't trying to work out a human solution to a problem. True wisdom is looking at the Bible and doing what it requires in order to solve the problem. True might doesn't come from going to a gym and pumping iron. True might comes from being absolutely confident that the position you are defending is a biblical one, not just a man-pleasing one. And, none of this—wisdom, might, understanding, what have you—can be obtained without the work of the Holy Spirit in our lives to bring it about. Just like Jesus!

We should examine another area of Jesus' life, this time at the beginning point of his vocation. It took place during his baptism at the hands of John the Baptist. A quick aside here: please understand that the baptism of John the Baptist was *not* the same thing as Christian baptism. Christian baptism is a sign and seal of a person entering into a covenant relationship with God. John was doing "his thing" before Jesus changed that sign and seal from circumcision (in the Old Testament) to baptism. That took place in Matthew 28, at the end of his life.

Rather, the baptism of John was to prepare the way for Jesus—to get the attention of the people of Israel that the Messiah, who would himself institute true baptism, was coming. We see this in the words of Luke 3:21-22 as we try to understand what happened when Jesus had John perform his baptism. *"Now when all the people were baptized, and when Jesus also had been baptized and was praying, the heavens were opened, [22]and the Holy Spirit descended on him in bodily form, like a dove; and a voice came from heaven, 'You are my beloved Son; with you I am well pleased.' "*

You see, Jesus didn't need this baptism so he could repent of sins, as others did. Jesus had no sins that required repentance. Jesus needed this baptism—which is to say, Jesus needed this work of the Holy Spirit—to consecrate and empower him for his vocation, for his public ministry.

In fact, his very first act of ministry following his baptism was reading the Scriptures at the synagogue in Nazareth. Think about the verses Jesus chose to read. They come from Isaiah 61:1-2, but Luke records the event in his gospel at 4:18-19. *"The Spirit of the Lord is upon me, because he has anointed me to proclaim good news to the poor. He has sent me to proclaim liberty to the captives and recovering of sight to the blind, to set at liberty those who are oppressed, to proclaim the year of the Lord's favor."* Clearly, Jesus needed the work of the Holy Spirit in his life to anoint him, to empower him to fulfill his vocation as the Messiah. But how in the world does this apply to you and me? We are far from being anything like a Messiah!

Well, just how different are we, really? After all, what does "Messiah" (or to use the Greek word for the same term, "Christ") really mean? The simple translation of both words is "an anointed one." What, you say you aren't anointed? Well, perhaps that's because so many people don't sense much fulfillment from their vocations, or because they do not realize that they need this anointing. Which, to put it in its simplest terms, means we need the work of the Holy Spirit in our vocations.

In order to do *any* vocation well, or even moderately well, one can't do it on his own. Every teacher, every mechanic, every student, every engineer, every nurse, every guard, every housewife, every contractor, every accountant, every *whatever-you-might-be* needs the work of the Holy Spirit to enable you to do your job well.

The anointing of the Holy Spirit is not just something that ministers, or preachers, need. No indeed—it is for everyone—no matter what your calling from God might be. Through prayer, through understanding how the Bible applies to your vocation, through fellowship with other Christians going through the same experiences, you need the filling of the Holy Spirit in order to succeed in whatever you may end up doing.

There is one final area of Jesus' life to examine to see how he needed the work of the Holy Spirit. It's not the resurrection—that was totally a miracle. You and I will all enjoy that work of the Holy Spirit, with no effort at all on our part, when we live in the new heavens and the new earth.

No, the area of Jesus' life I want to mention now is his death. While chapter after chapter of the New

Testament deals with this event, let's read just one verse from Hebrews, in chapter 9, verse 14. *"...How much more will the blood of Christ, who through the eternal Spirit, offered himself without blemish to God, purify our conscience from dead works to serve the living God."*

First of all, please notice that Jesus needed the work of the Holy Spirit to enable him to go to the cross to die for us, to provide the sacrifice for sins that you and I have committed. This act of redemption is, of course, the very heart of the gospel. Every single person needs to acknowledge that he is indeed a sinner and is unable to save himself from the penalty of sin that is eternal death and damnation.

Most of us don't like ever to admit we made a mistake or are guilty of anything. But in order to be in a right relationship with God we have got to get past this pride and humbly confess *all* of our sins. Then, and only then, will the shed blood of Jesus *"purify our conscience from dead works to serve the living God."*

But now, take this one step further. Let's assume for a moment that everyone reading this book is already a Christian. You have been saved by the blood, right? You have been born again, agreed? You are going to heaven, hallelujah?

But so what? You didn't do anything to achieve that status at all! Your redemption is none of your doing—it is all of God! Oh, sure, the Holy Spirit applied all of that work to your life, but you didn't do a thing on your own part to earn it or deserve it.

So, tell me please, how is it that we can draw an analogy of the work of the Holy Spirit in Jesus presenting his sacrifice on the cross to our lives today? We've done that with the other elements of his life. How does this one work? Let's go back to the very end of Hebrews 9:14 one more time. What did Jesus do for us? He *"purif[ied] our conscience from dead works to serve the living God."*

Jesus' work in our lives is not simply a fire insurance policy to save us from the deadly heat of hell. Jesus' death on the cross didn't just pay for a one-way ticket to heaven when we die. Jesus has redeemed us so that we—in this life—in the here and now, today—can *"serve the living God."* This means that each and every Christian (and if you included yourself in the assumption, that means *you*) must be involved in *"serving the living God."*

How do we serve God? How do we provide service on behalf of the God who has both created us and saved us? Actually, there are many ways we can do that. In Luke 4:8, in responding to one of Satan's temptations, Jesus said this, *"It is written, 'You shall worship the Lord your God, and him only shall you serve.'"* Here Jesus is making a connection between service and worship.

So if you want to serve God better in response to all he has done for you, one thing you *really* need to be doing is worshipping God regularly with all your heart, mind, soul and strength. Worship is not simply something nice to do; it is vital to your very well being. It is the heart of the service that we are to render to our God. If you are not worshipping God regularly, you are not serving God.

If you were to run a word study of the words "serve"; "service"; and "servant" just in the New Testament you would find dozens and dozens of occurrences. Without taking the time to list them all, let's examine a few of the ways we are taught in the Bible that we can serve God. Matthew 6:24 makes us aware that we serve God by not serving money; in other words, by practicing sound financial principles in our lives.

Matthew 24 and 25 contain parables teaching us our responsibility of taking care of God's household. That is, we serve God through our volunteering to do work in the church. If you're not helping out at church, your service to God is lacking.

John 12:26 instructs us that we serve God by following Jesus, which is to say, being aware of and following both the model of his life and his teachings of both faith and practice.

Acts 6:2 urges that we serve God by being involved in "mercy ministries," which means taking care of worldly needs of people both in the Church and in the world.

In 1 Corinthians 12:5, we find we serve God in a variety of opportunities, where we present the gospel to people to whom we are providing mercy ministries.

In 2 Corinthians 9:12-13 we are told that the cheerful giving of our tithes, plus offerings to God's work over and above our tithes, is in fact service to him.

Finally, Matthew 20:26 teaches us that the end result for those who are committed to the service of God is that they become the people who are considered the greatest in the kingdom of God.

I hope you can see that linkage. Jesus sacrificed his life in order that—we not only might be saved—but also that we might be in a position to offer service to God. And if Jesus needed the work of the Holy Spirit in his life to make his great sacrifice, how much more do we mere mortals need the work of the Spirit to enable us to give back to God our sacrifice of service.

I realize these first four chapters been foundational for the most part. We've seen how the Holy Spirit has been at work elsewhere—in the world, in the inspiration of the Bible, and in the life of Jesus. But starting in Chapter Five, we will examine how the Holy Spirit works directly in our lives—beginning with the primary work of regeneration.

¹Now there was a man of the Pharisees named Nicodemus, a ruler of the Jews. ²This man came to Jesus by night and said to him, "Rabbi, we know that you are a teacher come from God, for no one can do these signs that you do unless God is with him." ³Jesus answered him, "Truly, truly, I say to you, unless one is born again he cannot see the kingdom of God." ⁴Nicodemus said to him, "How can a man be born when he is old? Can he enter a second time into his mother's womb and be born?" ⁵Jesus answered, "Truly, truly, I say to you, unless one is born of water and the Spirit, he cannot enter the kingdom of God. ⁶That which is born of the flesh is flesh, and that which is born of the Spirit is spirit. ⁷Do not marvel that I said to you, 'You must be born again.' ⁸The wind blows where it wishes, and you hear its sound, but you do not know where it comes from or where it goes. So it is with everyone who is born of the Spirit."

John 3:1-8

Chapter Five
The Holy Spirit and Regeneration

What do you think is the one thing that people need more than anything else? Certainly, lots of different people have different ideas. Those who take introductory Psychology classes learn about a famous theory known as Maslow's Hierarchy of Needs. A psychiatrist named Maslow wrote a famous book in which he outlined a series of needs that people have, beginning with the most basic and then going up in the hierarchy.

Basic, bottom line needs, said Maslow, were those of the necessities of life: food, water, oxygen, etc. Anything a person needs to survive. I would suspect that the majority of those reading this chapter don't struggle much in this area. We might like to be better off than we are, but our most basic needs are met, so we can move up to the next level.

These involve safety needs: security, stability, protection, the need for structure, law and order (things like that). I live in a very small town in a very rural part of Virginia. Those of us, who live in small-town America rather than in large cities, generally enjoy the other safety needs, as well. But for those who live in the large cities, there is frequently some struggle in this category.

Maslow says that next come belongingness and love. If you listen to much of the pop music of recent years, you would think that was the most important, basic need people have. "All you need is love," one group sings. "People who need people are the luckiest people in the world," sings another person. In fact, it is by plucking the heartstrings of this need area that many TV sitcoms have become so popular over the years. This may be the area in which large majorities of Americans suffer. With broken marriages and estranged family members, belongingness and love are frequently problem areas—especially for children.

What about the next level? Self-esteem needs. That might be the top need in America right now. At least, you would think so if you go to bookstores in the malls and see shelf after shelf after shelf of "self-help" books covering just about every area of life. The need that Americans have for achievement and status are overwhelming. Without achieving these needs, many people feel inferior and helpless.

Maslow has one other level—and it is a level that he says very few people ever reach. He calls it "self-actualization." In simple terms, it means that people have to do what people have to do. Musicians must make music, artists must paint and poets must write if ultimately they are to be at peace with themselves. What humans can be, they must be.

You have to give Maslow a lot of credit for figuring out some basic needs of human nature. But, like so many other psychiatrists of his era, he was an atheist. So he left out of his formula the one greatest need—the need that, once fulfilled, takes a person straight to the top of the hierarchy. The most important thing every person needs is not to be self-actualized—the most important thing that every person needs is to be born again! At least, that's what Jesus says!

During his lifetime, Jesus taught people that there were a number of different things they must *do*. He said they must worship God. He said they must be servants. He said they must forgive those who sin against us. He said they must proclaim the gospel to all nations.

All of these things are important for every one of us to *do*. But it is what we must first *be* that is the top priority. Because without first *being* born again, we cannot *do* any of those other important things.

Chapter 3 of the Gospel of John is one of the best-known passages of the Bible, involving a conversation that Jesus had one night with a fellow named Nicodemus. It is in this chapter that Jesus teaches his followers that every person must be *"born again."* Born again is the biblical language for what theologians call Regeneration. You can see why, can't you? "To generate" is to be "born"—and "re" means "again." Born again—regeneration—same thing.

In this chapter of the book, we want to learn what the role of the Holy Spirit is in the work of regeneration. But first, we need to review a little of what we have learned in the earlier chapters. We must remind ourselves of the reason that every human has this need to be born again. That reason is that we are all sinners.

Remember what Paul said in 1 Corinthians 2:14. *"The natural person does not accept the things of the Spirit of God..."* Because of sin, we are born with intellects that cannot understand anything about the God who created us. Jesus himself said, in John 8:34, *"Truly, truly, I say to you, everyone who commits sin is a slave to sin."* Sin has such a powerful effect in our lives that left to our own, we are slaves to it—we can't do anything else but sin. It is so bad, Paul tells us in Romans 8:7, that we go so far as even hating God. *"For the mind that is set on the flesh is hostile to God, for it does not submit to God's law; indeed, it cannot."*

Sin affects us totally, in every aspect of our lives, in everything we do. Because of sin, we have no hope to achieving any of Maslow's hierarchy of needs— except maybe for food and shelter and outward safety. However, even animals can achieve that. We can't find freedom from fear and anxiety. We can't find true, lasting love and belonging. We can't reach any level of self-esteem. And we certainly can't be what we were meant to be.

Most of us, left on our own, trying to understand what life is all about, are just like poor Nicodemus. He couldn't figure it out either. Nicodemus was a highly religious man. He was a Pharisee—among the most learned religious scholars of his day. In our day and age, he would be a seminary professor, or a least a Bible college teacher. He read the Scriptures and thought he understood them. But one night, for reasons we are not told, but can only assume, he went to see Jesus.

This going out at night is highly unusual. People today often have night meetings, but back in those days, night was a time to be home with family. Nicodemus must have had an important reason to go out at night—and most Christian writers believe he didn't want his fellow Pharisees to see him talk to Jesus. In the daylight, Jesus and the Pharisees had a lot of confrontations, and the Pharisees would try to trip Jesus up, but he would always get the best of them. Nicodemus probably didn't want his peers to believe that he thought highly of Jesus, thus the night meeting.

The conversation is a bit strange at the beginning. Nicodemus shows up and the first thing he does is acknowledge what no other Pharisee is willing to acknowledge in public. *"This man came to Jesus by night and said to him, 'Rabbi, we know that you are a teacher come from God, for no one can do these signs that you do unless God is with him'"* (John 3:2). It is clear that Nicodemus is trying to talk to Jesus about whether or not he is the promised Messiah that the Scriptures he had studied and taught had been speaking about for many centuries. Nicodemus wanted to talk Bible.

But in his very unexpected response, Jesus made it clear that Nicodemus wasn't ready to talk Bible. Sure, he may have been a Bible college or seminary teacher, but he wasn't ready to talk Bible. He didn't really understand the Bible. Something more important, more basic had to happen to Nicodemus before the conversation could go on. We see that in verse 3, *"Jesus answered him, "Truly, truly, I say to you, unless one is born again he cannot see the kingdom of God."* Jesus frequently used the terminology "kingdom of God" when he was speaking of spiritual things, of biblical teaching. So one correct paraphrase of what Jesus said to him would be, "Unless one is born again he cannot understand the Bible."

Do you remember what we read from Paul's letter to the Corinthians a few minutes ago? It's in 1 Corinthians 2:14. Here is the whole verse again. *"The natural person does not accept the things of the Spirit of God, for they are folly to him, and he is not able to understand them because they are spiritually discerned."* In other words, Jesus is telling Nicodemus that there's no way he could talk about the Bible because he was still a natural man, and like all natural men, he was unable to understand spiritual things because he didn't have the work of the Holy Spirit in his life to "illumine" him so he could understand.

Pretty simple logic, isn't it? Nicodemus couldn't talk Bible with Jesus because he didn't have the work of the Holy Spirit in his life. So—Jesus said he first needed to get the work of the Holy Spirit in his life. This is to say, he must be born again because the work of regeneration is the work of the Holy Spirit. There is nothing you or I could do about being born the first time (*"of water,"* as Jesus puts it in John 3:5, or *"of flesh,"* as he puts it in verse 6). That took the action of our natural mother and father—we were just along for the ride.

It is the same with being born the second time, or being born *"of the Spirit,"* as Jesus refers to it in verses 6 and 7. We have nothing at all to do with that second birth, either. That's what Jesus is getting at in verse 8. *"The wind blows where it wishes, and you hear its sound, but you do not know where it comes from or where it goes. So it is with everyone who is born of the Spirit."*

Remember we saw in Chapter Three that the words "wind" and "spirit" are exactly the same words. That is true both in Greek and in Hebrew. Many times

Jesus uses the terminology of "wind" to describe the work of the Holy Spirit. You and I have no power over what the wind does to us and around us. In fact, we can't even see the wind itself when it is blowing. All we can see is the result of it.

It's just like that with the Holy Spirit coming to us in his great work of regeneration, of bringing us to the point of being born again. The Bible never tells us how the Holy Spirit does his work. We can't see him doing the work. All we can see is the result. You and I must see the result of regeneration in our lives if we want to have any kind of assurance that we belong to Jesus and are going to heaven. Regeneration is the first, essential, spiritual thing that happens to anyone who becomes a Christian.

Of course, not everyone teaches that regeneration comes first. A church with which I am personally acquainted had been looking for a pastor for almost two years. They were close to being desperate. Several of the people in the church knew a Methodist minister who seemed as if he would be interested. The Pulpit Committee asked him to interview; he did, and the congregation called him to be their pastor. But that created a big problem— because this gentleman was a Methodist minister, not a Presbyterian minister—and he did not believe the same things that Presbyterians believe. When a member of the Presbytery (the regional group of churches that is responsible for examining and credentialing ministers) was asked to talk to the possible pastor about theology and see if he could pass the examination in Presbytery, he asked one question. This question immediately shows whether a person can pass an exam as a Presbyterian minister.

That question was this: Which comes first—faith or regeneration? The immediate response was, "Oh, why faith, of course." The man believed (sincerely and honestly, for that was what he had always been taught) that an individual had to develop faith in Jesus, and if that faith were real enough and strong enough, then the Holy Spirit would come to regenerate him.

But that is not what was believed by the great leaders of the Protestant Reformation—by Martin Luther and John Calvin and John Knox and all the others. That is a key issue that separates Reformation theology (or Reformed theology, as it is known today), from others. Because Presbyterians (and many other groups that adhere to Reformed theology) believe that, it is absolutely clear, regeneration comes first— and that without being born again, one cannot have faith and repentance.

Let's look at one of the classic passages of the Bible (and believe me, there are many others) that teach this truth. It's Ephesians 1:3-6. *"Blessed be the God and Father of our Lord Jesus Christ, who has blessed us in Christ with every spiritual blessing in the heavenly places, [4]even as he chose us in him before the foundation of the world, that we should be holy and blameless before him. In love [5]he predestined us for adoption through Jesus Christ, according to the purpose of his will, [6]to the praise of his glorious grace, with which he has blessed us in the Beloved."*

It is the consistent teaching of the Apostle Paul, here and throughout his writings, that you and I did nothing on our own to become Christians. Rather, God *"chose us...before the foundation of the world,"* and *"predestined us."*

You and I don't just make a simple decision to become Christians, to be born again—that's God decision, God's choice. That's one of the reasons that many of us who believe Reformed theology do not practice the "invitation system" in preaching. We don't want to leave the impression that someone can make a "decision" to follow Christ and demonstrate that "decision" by answering an "invitation."

We are not able, without the initial work of the Holy Spirit, to make any spiritual decision. In fact, not only can we not understand spiritual things, not only are we slaves to sin, not only are we hostile towards God—we are in fact spiritually dead! Spiritually speaking, you and I are corpses. Ephesians 2:1 puts it this way: *"And you were dead in the trespasses and sins."* We are not just limited and weak. Spiritually speaking, we are dead. We are one of those corpses you see in TV programs that feature medical examiners and crime scene investigators. How in the world can a corpse make a decision to trust in Jesus? Well, it can't. And that's exactly why Jesus responded to Nicodemus the way he did.

Remember, in John 3:2, Nicodemus comes out and starts to talk about whether Jesus is the Messiah or not. What did Jesus say? Did he say, "Look, Nicodemus, I'm proud of you? You've got just enough spiritual knowledge almost to figure this out. All you have to do now is just believe that I am the Messiah, and you'll be OK. You express your faith in me, and I'll fix you up with everything else you need." No, that's not what Jesus said.

Jesus said, "Look, Nicodemus, you've got a big problem. No sense talking about whether or not I'm the Messiah promised in the Bible. You must solve your first problem. You are spiritually dead. You are a corpse. So your basic need is this: You must be born again!" That is everyone's basic need. That is your basic need; that is my basic need. That is the first thing, spiritually speaking, that must happen in your life. You, too, must be born again.

How do you know if you are born again or not? Well, look at your life. Are the results of regeneration there? Has your heart (not just some of your actions)—has your heart been changed? In his great prayer of repentance, King David cried out, *"Create in me a clean heart, O God, and renew a right spirit within me"* (Psalm 51:10). That's where you start—you cry out to God to create this new, clean heart in you—to renew this new, right spirit in you. In other words, you cry out to God to cause you to be born again. Tell him that you recognize you can do nothing on your own—only God, through his Holy Spirit can do it in you. And then you look for the changes in your heart. You look for assurances that your heart has been changed. (1 John 5:11-12)

Jesus described the unsaved, "un-born again" person this way in Mark 7:21-23. *"...Out of the heart of man, come evil thoughts, sexual immorality, theft, murder, adultery, coveting, wickedness, deceit, sensuality, envy, slander, pride, foolishness. All these evil things come from within, and they defile a person."* So, you look at your heart and see if new and different things are coming out, things that weren't there before—like honesty, patience and humility. If you find that, you love Jesus as you never have before, if your heart has been changed, then you have been born again.

My prayer is that each and every person who reads this book would know—for sure, with assurance—that you have been born again. I pray that you would have a new understanding of spiritual things and that the Holy Spirit has given you the gifts of faith and repentance. For that is one of the greatest works—perhaps even *the* greatest work—that the Holy Spirit is called upon to do.

I also pray that you would know that even though you aren't yet perfect,—because none of us are in this life (and that will be the topic of Chapter Six)—you have been changed. You have been born again. Because as Jesus said in John 3:3, *"...Unless one is born again he cannot see the kingdom of God."* Unless you are born again, you cannot understand spiritual things. And unless you are born again, you cannot go to heaven. The only other choice is "not so hot"—but it's a very hot one!

[12]Therefore, my beloved, as you have always obeyed, so now, not only as in my presence but much more in my absence, work out your own salvation with fear and trembling, [13]for it is God who works in you, both to will and to work for his good pleasure. [14]Do all things without grumbling or questioning, [15]that you may be blameless and innocent, children of God without blemish in the midst of a crooked and twisted generation, among whom you shine as lights in the world, [16]holding fast to the word of life, so that in the day of Christ I may be proud that I did not run in vain or labor in vain.

Philippians 2:12-16

Chapter Six
The Holy Spirit and Sanctification

How often do you think about sin? I'm not asking about the theory of sin now. I am asking how often do you think about the actuality of sin in your own personal life? Some people never think about sin. Either they don't believe in God, or they have a very faulty view of God and think that behavior is all just relative and that God loves everybody alike.

Some people who believe in both God and the existence of sin, still seldom think of their own sin. Oh, they might think of it briefly if they are involved in some really serious offense—but they somehow block the idea that what they are doing is indeed sinful.

Not long ago, the police in a major U.S. city arrested a pastor in a sting operation aimed at child pornographers. Apparently, this fellow got involved in Internet pornography, and then child pornography, and then in sexual chat rooms with very young girls. He was arrested as he went to a park where he expected to meet what he thought was one of these young girls—but it turned out to be a police detective instead.

Even upon his arrest, the pastor was in denial about his sinful activities. All he wanted to talk about was how horrible the police were and how illegal this sting operation had been. To make matters worse, he won his criminal court case! He beat the rap on a technicality, which just served to harden his denial of sin in his life.

Others may not deny sin in their lives, but when they are in the act of committing what they clearly know to be sin, they will only briefly think about it, and then somehow try to explain it away. They say things like, "Well, I really deserve this!" (That used to be one of my personal favorites.) Or, "God wants me to be happy, doesn't he?" Or, "This isn't as bad as a lot of other people's sin." If you fall into one of those categories and don't see anything wrong, then you're not going to get much out of this chapter. You won't see your need to do something about the sin in your life.

But perhaps you don't fall into one of those categories I've just mentioned. You are very aware of sin in your life. When you hear a sermon about sin, it affects you emotionally. When you read the Bible in your daily devotionals and are confronted with sin in your life, again you are affected. As a Christian, you really want to do something about sin in your life, *but* you are never quite sure what you should do to successfully deal with that sin.

If that is the case, then this chapter on "The Holy Spirit and Sanctification" is exactly what you need to understand. While Sanctification is another five-syllable theological term, it is not hard to understand. Sanctification is simply the ongoing process of overcoming sin in the life of a Christian. Let me repeat that. Sanctification is simply the ongoing process of overcoming sin in the life of a Christian. If you are serious about wanting to overcome sin in your life—than you *really* need to understand how sanctification works.

The first step in overcoming sin is to acknowledge its reality in your life. If anyone reading this holds to one of those categories I just discussed, then you will never be successful in overcoming sin. You must first acknowledge its reality. Even the great Apostle Paul understood the reality of sin in his life. In Romans 7 he wrote, *"...For I do not do what I want, but I do the very thing I hate."* (v. 15)

So important is the need to acknowledge the reality of sin in our lives, the Apostle John wrote in 1 John 1:8-10, *"If we say we have no sin, we deceive ourselves, and the truth is not in us. ⁹If we confess our sins, he is faithful and just to forgive us our sins and to cleanse us from all unrighteousness. ¹⁰If we say we have not sinned, we make him a liar, and his word is not in us."* In other words you have no hope whatsoever to have your sins forgiven and to be cleansed from all unrighteousness if you do not acknowledge and confess the fact that you are a sinner—not just in theory—but in actual, daily practice.

OK, you say you do so acknowledge and confess—what next? Well, before we look at the biblical solution for how to overcome sin in our lives (which is sanctification, right?), we must first look at a couple of false solutions that have been very popular over the years—to make sure we don't fall into the same mistaken ways of thinking.

The first false solution I would call the neo-Puritan way. It is not the way the original Puritans taught and practiced, but in the early days of America, there were many who believed and tried to fight sin with all their might and strength. They believed that sanctification is totally up to man to bring about.

Old Ben Franklin recorded in his autobiography how he tried to improve himself by making a daily checklist of all his bad habits. His theory was that if we simply know what is right, and use our reason and resolutions, we can conquer sin by our own strength and power. But his theory didn't work. His list just kept getting longer!

Well, if working as hard as you can to stop sin doesn't solve the problem—maybe the opposite idea will work. That was the famous position of a large group of Christians in the 19th century (and still continues to some extent today). They proclaimed, "Do not fight sin at all." These folks were fine

Christians, truly born-again and otherwise well meaning. Many of them gathered at an annual conference in the town of Keswick, England, so they carried the title, The Keswick Movement. Some were known as Victorious Life Christians.

They would teach things like, "deliverance from sin is not attained by struggle and painful effort, (or) by earnest resolution and self-denial." In this, they were correct! Man cannot overcome sin on his own effort. But then, they would go on to say things such as the published statements in the Clarion Classic entitled, "The Victorious Life." Its unknown author wrote, "Let go and let God!" "If it isn't easy, it isn't good." "If you have to work for the victory, it isn't the real thing." "We must not try not to sin."

Their error was to believe that sanctification was something that only God was involved in. "The potter must do all the work," they said. But what many people found out was that if they just tried to let the potter do all the work, the poor clay pot just kept crumbling. So many people in this Victorious Life movement went on to something new in the 20th Century. They began to teach and stress the need for some sort of second blessing from God. That in order to be a "sanctified Christian" you needed an additional, distinct work from God *after* he did his work of regeneration to save you. Sometimes this second blessing was to include Pentecostal gifts such as speaking in tongues. We will examine this aspect later in this volume.

Both of these proposed solutions to victory over sin are less than biblical. Man will never find holiness only by striving with might in his own strength. Something else is needed—supernatural help! But neither will man gain the victory simply by relying on supernatural help alone. The victory over sin—the process of sanctification—only happens by the combination of the two. The biblical solution to sanctification is God's working in us and our working, too.

When you are regenerated, when you are born again—the Holy Spirit comes to you to do this great work—and then he remains in you. He in fact dwells in you. See how Jesus himself explains it. In John 15:5, he says, *"I am the vine; you are the branches. Whoever abides in me and I in him, he it is that bears much fruit, for apart from me you can do nothing."* Then a bit later in John 17:21, he puts it this way. *"That they may all be one, just as you, Father, are in me, and I in you, that they also may be in us, so that the world may believe that you have sent me."*

You see, the indwelling of the Holy Spirit in the Christian's life brings about what we call the "mystical union with Christ." We are united to him in such a way that Jesus speaks of his actually being in us. Of course, we know he is physically located in heaven, so this is just a metaphor. But the Holy Spirit is not in a human body as Jesus is. The Spirit is not bound by space, so he is the one that actually dwells in us, just as God the Father and God the Son sent him to do. He is really there. The Holy Spirit provides our "mystical union" with Jesus.

So, it is the working together of the Holy Spirit in us, and our following the leading of the Holy Spirit to live a Christian life, that results in our sanctification and brings us true victory over sin. In the Bible, we are told this in 1 John 5:4. *"For everyone who has been born of God overcomes the world. And this is the victory that has overcome the world—our faith."* Paul says in Romans 6:14, *"For sin will have no dominion over you, since you are not under law but under grace."*

Do you ever wonder what those passages mean? Are they implying that every Christian has the victory over sin? Perhaps you have struggled with those passages, as I have. It may seem at times that you have *no* hope of victory and you are more the victim of sin rather than the victor over it. Yet, if you are born again of the Spirit of God and thereby united to Jesus, you cannot give up completely to sin. The Bible says you are *dead* to sin. A particular sin may conquer temporarily and in different ways, but ultimately, through the power of the Holy Spirit, it shall be completely eradicated. Satan has been given a mortal blow—his doom is sure. But in the meantime, he goes down fighting, still roaring.

Let me try to illustrate it this way. In August of 1945, the Japanese government signed a peace treaty aboard the USS *Missouri* in Tokyo Bay. World War II was finally over. America had the victory. But even after the peace treaty had been signed and the bulk of the Japanese army had surrendered, there were some soldiers—in fact quite a few—who kept fighting when American attempted to occupy many of the Pacific Islands.

In fact, in the mid 60s (nearly 20 years later), when I was living on the island of Guam in the mid-Pacific Marianas Islands, there were still Japanese soldiers hiding in caves just over the edge of the cliff at the end of the main runway at Anderson Air Force Base. Some of the servicemen even put food out in the evening so they wouldn't starve to death!

That's the way it is in the life of everyone who is mystically united with Jesus. The victory has been won. Satan and sin are defeated! It has already happened! Oh, there will still be guerrilla warfare carried on sporadically, and at times, it can take on great proportions, but the victory is sealed.

The peace treaty with God has been signed with the blood of Jesus himself. It is only a matter of time before the last vestige of sin will be done away with.

In this biblical sense, it is possible to speak of the victorious life as the Apostle John does in 1 John 5:4.

Now, how does this process of sanctification work? In the preceding chapter, we had to say that we had *no* information on how regeneration works. But on this topic, we have a little more data to go on. In reviewing this material, we will just mention and paraphrase it.

To begin with, sanctification is primarily the work of the Holy Spirit. Peter tells us in his first letter that the Holy Spirit is called the Spirit of sanctification. Paul says in Romans 8 that we are "led by the Spirit." We'll talk more about this process in a later chapter when we deal with the issue of guidance. Both John and Paul also remind us that the Holy Spirit is the one who dwells in us (John 14:17, Romans 8:9). So clearly, the work of sanctification is the work of the Holy Spirit as he functions as an essential part of the life of every Christian.

We also know that sanctification is a gradual process. No one just becomes sanctified overnight, and then stays that way forever. Peter tells us in 2 Peter 3 that we are to grow in both grace and knowledge. Obviously growing signifies an ongoing process.

When does this process end? Well take note of this small part of the description of what heaven is like as John tells us in Revelation 21:27. *"But nothing unclean will ever enter it, nor anyone who does what is detestable or false, but only those who are written in the Lamb's book of life."* You see—complete sanctification, perfection if you will—does not come until we arrive in heaven.

But this process, this growth, involves both the Holy Spirit and you. Instead of explaining this statement again, this time let me just list several crucial verses, which I hope are some that are already familiar. Romans 12:1-2 urges, *"I appeal to you therefore, brothers, by the mercies of God, to present your bodies as a living sacrifice, holy and acceptable to God, which is your spiritual worship. ²Do not be conformed to this world, but be transformed by the renewal of your mind, that by testing you may discern what is the will of God, what is good and acceptable and perfect."*

Ephesians 6:11-12 instructs us, *"Put on the whole armor of God, that you may be able to stand against the schemes of the devil. ¹²For we do not wrestle against flesh and blood, but against the rulers, against the authorities, against the cosmic powers over this present darkness, against the spiritual forces of evil in the heavenly places."*

We are encouraged in 1Timothy 6:12 to, *"Fight the good fight of the faith. Take hold of the eternal life to which you were called and about which you made the good confession in the presence of many witnesses."*

The Holy Spirit and Sanctification

Hebrews 12:1 says, *"Therefore, since we are surrounded by so great a cloud of witnesses, let us also lay aside every weight, and sin which clings so closely, and let us run with endurance the race that is set before us..."*

Did you notice all those imperative verbs? *"Present your bodies!" "Be transformed!" "Stand against the devil!" "Fight the good fight of faith!" "Lay aside every weight!" "Run the race!"* Isn't it obvious? Sanctification requires real work, real effort on our part. But at least we are not alone. The Holy Spirit is dwelling in us, guiding us, strengthening us. And we remember that the victory is already won!

Well then, why aren't we doing better at this sanctification stuff? Why do most Christians in America suffer from the effects of sin? Let me just quickly run down the Ten Commandments to prove this point. Think about how many professed Christians you know (perhaps including yourself) who are not just guilty—but are not even trying very hard to overcome one or more sins. Are they any of these?

- Failing to worship God

- Worshipping something or someone other than God

- Taking God's name in vain

- Profaning the Sabbath day

- Dishonoring parents and just about every other person in authority over you

- Murdering (especially those who take the lives of unborn babies, but especially those who fail to follow Jesus' instructions not to hate their brother)

- Committing adultery—and every other kind of sexual perversion you can think of

- Stealing—perhaps not with a gun, but with fraud, injustice, extortion, gambling, and on and on

- Lying—perhaps the most frequent sin in our lives

- Coveting—do you really want me to discuss the extent of materialism in the lives of Christians today?

So what good is all the theory we've just learned about sanctification? I don't want to leave you feeling more guilty for your sin than when you started this chapter! What are the practical implications of what we've learned about how sanctification works? How do we apply it to our lives?

Well, let's turn back to Philippians 2 and consider it one more time. Now that we have looked at how sanctification happens, maybe our newfound knowledge will make a bigger impact on us. Verses 12-16 reads, *"Therefore, my beloved, as you have always obeyed, so now, not only as in my presence but much more in my absence, work out your own salvation with fear and trembling, [13]for it is God who works in you, both to will and to work for his good pleasure. [14]Do all things without grumbling or questioning, [15]that you may be blameless and innocent, children of God without blemish in the midst of a crooked and twisted generation, among whom you shine as lights in the world, [16]holding fast to the word of life, so that in the day of Christ I may be proud that I did not run in vain or labor in vain."*

This working out of our salvation is in fact the work we do in sanctification, in dealing with sin in our lives. Yes, God works in us, but he doesn't do all the work for us. We've got our load to carry. And as we carry it, Paul says, we need to do it without grumbling or complaining. We need to hold fast to the word of life, as he puts it in verse 16. When we read in the word of God that something is sin, then we must be realistic and obey it—not try to slough it off, or make excuses.

And the presence of the Holy Spirit will indeed help us along the way. What we need is to utilize fully his help. We can do that in at least three ways. One, we should pray regularly for a fuller presence of the Holy Spirit in our lives. We will be spending an entire chapter on that topic a bit further on in the book. In the meantime, anytime you are asking God to forgive you of a sin and you want him to assist you to overcome it, be sure to ask for a filling of his Holy Spirit.

Two, we should not just depend on a sermon once a week to provide what we need from the Bible. We should privately and in small groups study and meditate on the word of God. Peter reminds us in 1 Peter 2:2 that we should, *"like newborn infants, long for the pure spiritual milk, that by it you may grow up..."* After all, Jesus himself said to God the Father in his prayer in John 17:19, *"...for their sake I consecrate myself, that they also may be sanctified in truth."* Clearly, sanctification comes about through the word of God.

And then, three, we can be more and more filled with the Holy Spirit by being faithful in worship. In Hebrews 10:25, we are warned that we should be *"not neglecting to meet together, as is the habit of some, but encouraging one another..."* Certainly, the time you spend together with other Christians as a congregation of God's people—singing praise, offering prayers, giving of yourselves in your tithes and offerings, and focusing on the teaching of the word of God are all positive ways to work out your salvation.

Sanctification is indeed the work of the Holy Spirit. God the Holy Spirit is involved at every step. God the

Holy Spirit gives us our own ability to participate in the process as we are commanded. Combine God's work and man's work—and the outcome are victory over sin. To be sure, on this side of heaven, sin will not be fully eradicated, but there will be a marked and definite progress toward sanctification. That combination will indeed result in a biblically victorious Christian life.

[1]Simeon Peter, a servant and apostle of Jesus Christ, to those who have obtained a faith of equal standing with ours by the righteousness of our God and Savior Jesus Christ: [2]May grace and peace be multiplied to you in the knowledge of God and of Jesus our Lord. [3]His divine power has granted to us all things that pertain to life and godliness, through the knowledge of him who called us to his own glory and excellence, [4]by which he has granted to us his precious and very great promises, so that through them you may become partakers of the divine nature, having escaped from the corruption that is in the world because of sinful desire. [5]For this very reason, make every effort to supplement your faith with virtue, and virtue with knowledge, [6]and knowledge with self-control and self-control with steadfastness, and steadfastness with godliness, [7]and godliness with brotherly affection, and brotherly affection with love. [8]For if these qualities are yours and are increasing, they keep you from being ineffective or unfruitful in the knowledge of our Lord Jesus Christ. [9]For whoever lacks these qualities is so nearsighted that he is blind, having forgotten that he was cleansed from his former sins. [10]Therefore, brothers, be all the more diligent to make your calling and election sure, for if you practice these qualities you will never fall. [11]For in this way there will be richly provided for you an entrance into the eternal kingdom of our Lord and Savior Jesus Christ. [12]Therefore I intend always to remind you of these qualities, though you know them and are established in the truth that you have. [13]I think it right, as long as I am in this body, to stir you up by way of reminder, [14]since I know that the putting off of my body will be soon, as our Lord Jesus Christ made clear to me. [15]And I will make every effort so that after my departure you may be able at any time to recall these things. [16]For we did not follow cleverly devised myths when we made known to you the power and coming of our Lord Jesus Christ, but we were eyewitnesses of his majesty. [17]For when he received honor and glory from God the Father, and the voice was borne to him by the Majestic Glory, "This is my beloved Son, with whom I am well pleased," [18]we ourselves heard this very voice borne from heaven, for we were with him on the holy mountain. [19]And we have something more sure, the prophetic word, to which you will do well to pay attention as to a lamp shining in a dark place, until the day dawns and the morning star rises in your hearts, [20]knowing this first of all, that no prophecy of Scripture comes from someone's own interpretation. [21]For no prophecy was ever produced by the will of man, but men spoke from God as they were carried along by the Holy Spirit.

2 Peter 1:1-21

Chapter Seven
The Holy Spirit and Guidance

D uring the period I was working on this chapter, there was a commercial running frequently on TV. It was for an office supply store and it would show all kinds of problems that needed solving (that needed guidance, if you will). A dad faced with simultaneously changing diapers on newborn twins. A doctor about to perform a surgical procedure never tried before. A middle school boy asked to solve a complex math problem. Once it was clear that the hapless star of the commercial was not able to accomplish the task, up would pop an "easy button." All the person had to do to reach his goal was push this easy button—and bingo, he received guidance, the problem was solved, the task was simplified, and everyone lived happily after.

It has been my experience that there are a lot of Christians out there who are looking for the easy button to solve problems in their lives. Among Christians, this happens most frequently when they are trying to receive guidance from God on what or how to do something. In fact, I can't think of many areas of the Christian life where there are more diverse approaches (and therefore more erroneous ways) to understand God and his word than in the area of guidance. (We'll take a look at several of those erroneous ways later in the chapter.) The bottom line is that the topic of the

Holy Spirit and Guidance is on one hand very simple (since there is only one proper way to receive guidance) and on the other hand very difficult—because so many of us would prefer to have an easy button.

It may not be an easy button, but God has given every Christian the ability to know the will of God for their life; he has given us guidance and it comes from but one source—the Bible, the word of God. Let's look first at 2 Timothy 3:15-16, *"...and how from childhood you have been acquainted with the sacred writings, which are able to make you wise for salvation through faith in Christ Jesus. [16]All Scripture is breathed out by God and profitable for teaching, for reproof, for correction, and for training in righteousness."*

Do you see it? The Scriptures have been *"breathed out by God."* (That's what it means to be inspired. You will recall we discussed that at length in the chapter on the Holy Spirit and the Bible. Because the Scriptures come directly from God, they have value. They are useful, even *"profitable for teaching, for reproof, for correction, and for training in righteousness."* Not only does the Bible show us the way of salvation through Jesus, it does so much more!

Paul speaks here of four different areas of our life in which the Scriptures guide us. First, they teach us. They show each Christian what he must believe and do. Second, they convict him of his failures to live up to the standard, which is to say they show him his sins. We looked at that in the chapter on the Holy Spirit and Regeneration. Third, they correct him. It's not enough to know what not to do; we must also know what we should do. And fourth, they train him in the disciplined ways of righteousness that God requires. (We covered this topic in the chapter on the Holy Spirit and Sanctification.)

Moreover, please notice that in the next verse, 2 Timothy 3:17, Paul says emphatically that the Bible is the only thing that one needs to become sanctified— *"that the man of God may be competent, equipped for every good work."* Peter makes exactly the same point at the beginning of his second letter. *"His divine power has granted to us [ALL] things that pertain to life and godliness, through the knowledge of him who called us to his own glory and excellence, [4]by which he has granted to us his precious and very great promises."* (2 Peter 1:3-4)

Notice I put the word "ALL" in full caps. This is crucial! God has given us everything we need for our life and for godliness. He has given it to us in his Word, in the Bible. We can know the will of God. We can receive guidance from God through the work of the Holy Spirit. We receive this guidance through the Spirit's work of illumination, enabling us to understand and apply what the Bible is teaching us.

Now—at this point we need to divide this topic into two separate, yet equally important, parts. The Bible gives us guidance both in moral issues (the things that are either right or wrong for Christians) and in practical issues (the things that are morally equal but one choice might be better than another might). Let's look first at the guidance we have in moral issues.

Some moral issues are crystal clear in the Bible. Do not murder. Do not lie. Do not covet. Remember the Sabbath Day. Honor your parents. Husbands love your wives. A Christian must never marry a non-Christian. What, you say, "Is that on the same level as the Ten Commandments? I thought that was just a suggestion." Actually, it is as much a moral imperative as any other part of the Moral Law of God. It just isn't given to us in a direct command.

When Paul writes in 1 Corinthians 7:39 that a woman who has been deserted by an unbelieving husband is free to remarry, but that the new marriage must be *"in the Lord,"* he is teaching a moral requirement. The implication is that the first marriage occurred when both were unbelievers. The woman later turned her life over to Jesus, but the husband did not and he ultimately deserted her for that reason. So the deduction to be made is that once a person is a Christian, then they may only marry *"in the Lord."* You see, it's not enough for one person entering into a marriage to be a Christian since in a marriage the two become one. It is that united one, the married couple, who must be *"in the Lord."*

As you can see, not every moral requirement is spelled out in detail. So Christians should be involved in constant reading and study of the Scriptures, so they have the ability to follow the illuminating work of the Holy Spirit in the area of guidance. If you can "by good and necessary consequence" (to use the language of the Westminster Confession of Faith, sections 1-6), properly deduce a principle from the Scriptures, it is just as valuable, just as much a moral obligation as one of the Ten Commandments.

At the same time we talk about the Holy Spirit working through his activity of illumination, we must be careful to understand that's as far as he goes. The Holy Spirit does not work apart from the word of God. He does not have a separate ministry of guidance of his own. Recently my wife and I were visiting a church that has a children's message. (My relating this story should in no way indicate my endorsement of that particular element of worship!) The lady offering the teaching that day on the topic of prayer asked them, "Does God speak to you when you pray?" And, as children all trying to give a correct answer without really understanding the underlying theology, they yelled in unison, "Yes!" The teacher responded. "That's right. The Holy Spirit speaks to us when we pray!"

I was able to limit my response to a quiet whisper in my wife's ear. "That's exactly why I dislike children's messages—the theology can be so terrible." You see, the truth is that the Holy Spirit does *not* speak to us when we pray. In fact, the Holy Spirit never "speaks" to us. Jesus never "speaks" to us. God the Father never "speaks" to us. God's way of communicating his will to us is—plain and simple—through the Bible. Oh, yes, the Holy Spirit is involved, but his work is that of illumination, not speaking. We'll talk more on this shortly, when we look at several of the erroneous ways in which Christians seek guidance.

First, however, we need to deal with guidance in areas where there are no moral absolutes. There are many times in our lives when we need guidance, when we need to know what God's will is, in areas in which we have two equally moral choices and need to decide between them. These are issues of Christian Liberty— where the two choices are presented, neither of which is specifically prohibited or required by the word of God. Although we can (and should) make the choice, we still can expect guidance from the Holy Spirit.

Again, an illustration is of great help. The same morning I heard the children's message mentioned above, the pastor was preaching and part of the application of his message was on guidance. He was speaking of a time when he and his wife had two equally valid options from which to pick. He was in seminary in the Boston area and his wife was accepted for a PhD program in Philadelphia. The question was—should they move to Philadelphia (where he could transfer to another fine seminary) or should they remain where they were until he finished his studies. They sought out counsel from their pastor. After an hour of talking with him, and his making charts of all the pros and cons, the pastor sat back in his chair and pronounced, "Well, neither choice is sinful, so you might as well just flip a coin!" Happily, the seminarian and his wife thought that wasn't quite right, and used another factor to make their decision. The condominium they would have bought in Philadelphia turned out to be one (they found out as they were reading the fine print in the contract) that did not accept pets. They had a dog and wanted to keep it. So they made the decision to remain in the Boston area.

That is an excellent illustration of the way in which God's Spirit will guide us to choose one decision over another. In every such case, we should approach it following the same three principles: study the choices to be made to be sure they are morally equal, pray that the Holy Spirit would strengthen our powers of deduction and rational thinking, and ask God to control all the circumstances involved. I think we can clearly say that God can help us make these decisions in even as mundane a way as saying our priority in this situation is to keep our family pet!

Even as we recognize that God works through circumstances, we must yet beware of an important limitation. It is also true that, since sin affects all of man's faculties, including our ability to reason, we can never say that a choice we make is an infallible one. Only time will allow us to judge the providence of God, and tell us whether the choice is the correct one for the long term. Unless we want to end up being so fearful of making the wrong choice we refuse to make a decision—then we must make our best, sanctified, rational judgment—make the choice and ask God to either bless it or lead us through circumstances to a different choice.

Another illustration might be helpful. One year it was time to trade in my older van that had gone well past the 100,000-mile mark and lacked the dependability I needed for the many miles I drove each year. I decided to trade it for a mid-size sport utility vehicle (SUV.) I was living in the mountains of Virginia and everyone around me had a truck or a SUV with 4-wheel drive, and it just made good, rational sense that I needed one too. So I bought one (used, of course, with about 12,000 miles on it—but that's another issue). Six months (and 30,000 miles) later, I came to the conclusion that I had made a wrong choice. The interior was smaller than my van; the seat height from the floor was about 2 inches lower than my van (which was not good for my chronic back injury), and the gas mileage was horrible. Through the circumstances of my discomfort, an increasingly painful back and an ever-larger crunch on my budget, I decided I had made the wrong choice and traded the

SUV for another van. Yes, it is certainly true that God guides us providentially even through some of the smallest possible details.

So, at the end of the day, we receive guidance from the Holy Spirit as he illuminates the Bible to help us understand what our moral obligations are, and then through assisting us to make rational choices between otherwise equal possibilities. But what do you do if you are not sure which choice to make? What do you do if your knowledge of the Bible is not mature enough to make you certain that one choice may not involve sin? Well, doesn't the Bible teach that, *"Whatever does not proceed from faith is sin?"* (Romans 14:23) Indeed it does. So if you have doubts, if you are not sure, then don't make that choice. Exercise the spiritual gift of patience and wait until you gain more understanding of the biblical teaching in that particular area in question, or until you receive providential guidance through circumstances in which God places you. Not all decisions have to be made immediately.

We want to conclude this chapter by looking at some important examples of just a few of the ways that Christians may err in seeking guidance from the Holy Spirit. These ways can be broadly divided into several categories. The first is to make the mistake to believe that there are sources of guidance that are valid in addition to Scripture.

The major illustration of this first category is the teaching of the Roman Catholic Church that the traditions of the Church are to be given equal weight with Scripture, and especially the view that when the Pope speaks *ex cathedra* his judgment is given equal weight with Scripture. This position was, of course, one of the major issues that brought the Reformation into existence. *Sola Scriptura* ("the Bible alone") became one of the hallmarks of the Reformation in opposition to these teachings of the Roman Catholic Church. Today we find the same problem with the Church of Jesus Christ of Latter Day Saints (the Mormons), who believe in other sources they set on equal footing with the Bible. No, only the Bible has infallible authority in the life of a Christian.

The second category is to make the mistake of believing that you can receive some sort of direct revelation from the Holy Spirit yourself. This category has historical roots in the medieval Church among those known as "mystics," but we also have plenty of current illustrations to help us understand it. In fact, the heart of the teaching of the traditional Pentecostal movement, which began in the early 20th Century, along with much of the current Charismatic movement, is that an individual can receive a direct revelation from God. Some believe this is a new revelation, in addition to the Scripture, but many believe it is simply in confirmation of the Scriptures. Most believe that it is received directly by the individual from the Holy Spirit.

Let's recall what we just learned from 2 Peter 1:3. God has already—in the past, through the Scriptures—given us "[ALL] *things that pertain to life and godliness.*" God has no need to give us new or direct revelation. He accomplished all of that for us in the work of the Holy Spirit in the inspiration and continuing illumination of the Scriptures. We are not to expect any new revelation from God. As we read our Bibles, the Lord often impresses upon us a new understanding and application of the word, but this is not a new "revelation." Personal application of the word is not revelation in the scriptural sense.

One final area among the common mistakes Christians make in the area of guidance is one I would call providential guidance. This would include a laundry list of illustrations—many based on historical incidents in the Bible, none of which is supported directly by the teaching of the Bible. It is important as we approach this category to remind ourselves of a major principle of biblical interpretation (or Hermeneutics, as the scholars refer to it). That is that you never draw a biblical teaching from a historical example or illustration. If the concept is not taught elsewhere didactically (where the Bible intends to teach us something), then it was not intended by God to become a principle.

Issues included in this list would be obvious things like consulting mediums or divining—but also would include the using of fleeces or the casting of lots. You see, a sovereign God controls all things in the world—including minute details in the lives of individuals. But it is God who has the control, not the circumstances or events in our lives. Because of this, we may never say the course of events shows us infallibly that God wants us to do or not to do a certain thing. Providence (which is the old-fashioned word Christians would use for what we simply call external circumstances) tells us only what God has done. We just can't infallibly determine what God wants us to do in the future by correctly observing providential happenings in the past.

Not only are these common mistakes in guidance *not* taught in the Bible, but when you take time to consider them carefully, they even tend to be irrational or arbitrary. Gideon knew that his use of fleeces was wrong. Let's look at this all-too familiar story again. It's in Judges 6:37-39. Gideon is speaking, *"...'behold, I am laying a fleece of wool on the threshing floor. If there is dew on the fleece alone, and it is dry on all the ground, then I shall know that you will save Israel by my hand, as you have said.' [38] And it was so. When he rose early next morning and squeezed the fleece, he wrung enough dew from the fleece to fill a bowl with water. [39] Then Gideon said to God, 'Let not your anger burn against me; let me speak just once more. Please let me test just once more with the fleece. Please let it be dry on the fleece only, and on all the ground let there be dew.'"*

Yes, God guided Gideon—supernaturally—through the fleece incident even though Gideon knew that it was a sin against God—that he demonstrated a lack of trust and would even anger God. God is sovereign, and he can (and will) do things the way he wants to do them, and you and I may never understand why. But we cannot establish a biblical principle from this providential act by God.

As another example, just because the replacement for Judas Iscariot to become the twelfth Apostle was accomplished by the casting of lots in Acts 1:26, that is not, in and of itself, a valid reason for us to seek guidance from God by casting lots today. It is quite interesting to note that this is the last historical occurrence of the casting of lots. No such event is described after Pentecost. Why, you ask? I would venture to say the implication of this fact (and perhaps even a good and necessary consequence) is that the Holy Spirit was poured on God's people at Pentecost and the principle of illumination of the Scriptures was firmly established. Thus, there is no need for any such providential or supernatural act for a Christian to receive guidance.

You and I already have (to repeat it one last time) "ALL *things that pertain to life and godliness*" (2 Peter 1:3) because you and I can depend on receiving guidance through the ongoing work of illumination of the Scriptures by God the Holy Spirit.

¹²So then, brothers, we are debtors, not to the flesh, to live according to the flesh. ¹³For if you live according to the flesh you will die, but if by the Spirit you put to death the deeds of the body, you will live. ¹⁴For all who are led by the Spirit of God are sons of God. ¹⁵For you did not receive the spirit of slavery to fall back into fear, but you have received the Spirit of adoption as sons, by whom we cry, "Abba! Father!" ¹⁶The Spirit himself bears witness with our spirit that we are children of God, ¹⁷and if children, then heirs—heirs of God and fellow heirs with Christ, provided we suffer with him in order that we may also be glorified with him.

Romans 8:12-17

Chapter Eight
The Holy Spirit and Assurance

We begin this chapter with a story about a famous Welsh hymn writer named William Cowper. (All Welshmen have names that are either impossible to pronounce or are pronounced differently than they look. This is pronounced "Cooper.") Cowper wrote many wonderful Christian hymns. Perhaps you recognize titles such as "O for a Closer Walk with God" or "The Spirit Breathes upon the Word." Cowper—who was a classically trained English poet as well as a lawyer—was responsible for the writing of over 300 hymns—all for a single hymnbook that was used for mid-week evangelistic services at John Newton's church in a small town in England. (Newton, who wrote "Amazing Grace" and "Glorious Things of Thee Are Spoken," was Cowper's pastor.)

Read words such as, "O for a closer walk with God, a calm and heav'nly frame, a light to shine upon the road that leads me to the Lamb!" Or, "Ye fearful saints, fresh courage take; the clouds ye so much dread, are big with mercy, and shall break, in blessings on your head." You would think that if there were anyone who had great assurance of his salvation, it would be William Cowper.

But the sad story of his life is one of depression, gloom and doubt. Just after finishing his training as a lawyer, he tried to commit suicide at least five times. Once he considered poison, but couldn't bring himself to put it in his mouth. Once he tried a knife, but the blade snapped. Three times, he tried to hang himself. Once an iron pin holding the rope broke, once the wooden crossbeam to which he had fastened the cord cracked and the third time the cloth noose tore, dropping him to the floor.

He underwent hospitalization for depression for nearly two years and then began worshipping at John Newton's church, where he wrote so many wonderful hymns. But the depression returned and he once again was convinced that he should end his life. He hired a coachman to drive him to the river so he might drown himself, but the darkness of night prevented the driver from finding his way and Cowper was returned to his doorstep. Aware that God had intervened, he wrote the words to his hymn, "God Moves in a Mysterious Way." Throughout his years, William Cowper suffered greatly from a lack of assurance of the work of God's grace in his life.

Our topic in this chapter is assurance. If there was ever a topic that divided Christian denominations and theological positions, it is the subject of assurance. There are two extremes on the topic, as there are on most theological issues. One extreme says, "Assurance? I don't think I could ever say that I *know* that I am saved. That would be presumptuous. I hope that I am, but I don't have any certainty about it." The other extreme would say, "Of course I have assurance that I am saved. I walked the aisle, didn't I? The preacher told me that all I needed to do is pray a prayer to receive Christ, and that once I did that I could have perfect assurance of my eternal security forever. I mean, it was promised to me by God, and he wouldn't lie, would He?"

Both of these extremes have problems. Both are contrary to historic, Reformation theology and biblical teaching and practice. The first denies the possibility of assurance—the Bible clearly teaches it is possible, desirable and even expected. The second fails to deal adequately with professions of faith in Jesus that appear to be genuine but are not.

To begin with, please have no doubt but that the Bible teaches us clearly that it *is* possible for a Christian to have assurance of grace and salvation. Most of you know that famous sentence from the lips of the Apostle Paul, found in 2 Timothy 1:12. *"...For I know whom I have believed, and I am convinced that he is able to guard until that Day what has been entrusted to me."* There were no doubts in Paul's mind about his assurance of salvation. He knew; he was convinced!

The same was true with the Apostle John. In fact, his entire letter of 1 John, was written just for the purpose of encouraging believers to find assurance of their salvation. Notice chapter 5, verse 13, *"I write these things to you who believe in the name of the Son of God that you may know that you have eternal life."*

While these verses from the Bible make it absolutely clear that Christians can and should have assurance of their salvation, there are some—in fact quite a few—who hold to a different theological viewpoint. Sometimes these two views are known for the names of the theologians who first verbalized them—John Calvin and Jacob Arminius. So the theological positions are sometimes referred to as Calvinism and Arminianism. But it's probably easier to remember these two variables by thinking of the key element of how one becomes a Christian. A Calvinist believes it is by the election of God—an Arminian believes it is by the free will of man.

When you look at both of these systems and examine what they teach about election or free will, it is quite obvious where the differences come from. If you believe you were saved solely by the grace of God, that God himself chose you *"before the foundations of the earth"* (Ephesians 1:4) to become a Christian, then of course you would believe that God would and could also provide assurance that you will always remain a Christian and that you will end up in heaven. Calvin called it the Perseverance of the Saints.

But if you believe, with Arminians, that your salvation is not the result of election, but is rather the result of exercising your own free will to make a decision to believe in Jesus, then it is consistent for you to believe that one cannot have assurance. If it required your decision first to believe, then it must be dependent upon your free will to continue to believe until the end—you might change your belief! Whether or not you are resolved not to do so, you are only human and therefore a sinner, so it might happen, based on circumstances, that you would change your mind.

Those two positions are, based on their initial premise, both arguable from Scripture. What you find rampant in America today, however, is a total aberration of either of the two positions. It is found throughout churches that practice what I would call decisional regeneration. In these churches, you find people preaching and teaching that it is up to man to make the decision to first believe, but from then on, God takes over and you can be absolutely sure of your eternal security—no matter what you do or how you live! Thus, the thinking is Arminian up to the point of becoming a Christian, and Calvinist from then on.

It is within these kind of churches that you end up with so very many people making an initial profession of faith, who are given what turns out to be false assurance about going to heaven, and then live any way they want to live—not going to church, not even trying to live outwardly as a Christian would live. This system of thinking has to devise some teaching to explain these people who made a decision to become a Christian, but live a non-Christian life.

Bill Bright, founder of Campus Crusade for Christ, tried to explain this inconsistency as Carnal Christianity. Bill, who is now deceased, changed his theological position on this late in his life, after sitting under the preaching of PCA ministers for nearly 15 years. He initially taught, however—and many, many still believe—that there is such a thing as a carnal Christian.

In fact, the theory says, there are three kinds of people in the world: non-Christians, carnal Christians and spiritual Christians. The spiritual Christian is one who goes to church and seeks to live a Christian life. The carnal Christian is one who once made a profession of faith, but no longer goes to church or seeks to live a Christian life but thinks that he is going to heaven (falsely so, because he is not truly saved). If he were truly a Christian, he would want to live a Christian life; he would have the desire to do so, or would be consciously bothered by the fact that he is not.

But Jesus knows of only two types of people in the world. He referred to them as sheep (his people, Christians) and goats (everyone else). Jesus taught of only two eternal destinations—heaven and hell. So clearly, those who believe that they are Christians, but do not desire to live like Christians, have no basis to think they are destined for heaven. In other words, they have no basis for eternal security.

This is because the Bible teaches quite a different thing about the basis for assurance of our salvation and our eternal destiny in heaven. To begin with, our assurance is based on God's promises, never on our decisions based on free will. As you read the following well-known passages of Scripture, notice what they are saying about the basis for assurance. Romans 8:1, 38-39 says, *"[1]There is therefore now no condemnation for those who are in Christ Jesus. ... [38]For I am sure that neither death nor life, nor angels nor rulers, nor things present nor things to come, nor powers, [39]nor height nor depth, nor anything else in all creation, will be able to separate us from the love of God in Christ Jesus our Lord."*

That was Paul. Now listen to the Apostle John in 1 John 5:11-12. *"And this is the testimony, that God gave us eternal life, and this life is in his Son. [12]Whoever has the Son has life; whoever does not have the Son of God does not have life."*

Could it be much clearer? God promises eternal life, God promises access to heaven forever—to those to whom he has given life by the regenerating work of the Holy Spirit. Not only does the Spirit's work of regeneration carry with it these great promises, the

Holy Spirit's ongoing work in the process of sanctification (which we examined in an earlier chapter) provides evidence of our being Christians. Look at Romans 8:13-14. *"¹³For if you live according to the flesh you will die, but if by the Spirit you put to death the deeds of the body, you will live. ¹⁴For all who are led by the Spirit of God are sons of God."*

The logic is pretty clear there, isn't it? If you are *"led by the Spirit"* (in other words, if you have been regenerated by the Spirit and the Spirit is dwelling in you) then you are God's son (in other words, you are a Christian). And you know that you are led by the Spirit by what? You know by making a decision to trust Jesus and then *"living according to the flesh"* like a so-called carnal Christian? *No!* If you do that, you will die, Paul says. Only those who *"put to death the deeds of the body"* (in other words, only those *in* the process of sanctification) are going to live eternally.

Just to emphasize the importance of this point, let me ask you to consider 1 John 2:3-5. *"And by this we know that we have come to know him, if we keep his commandments. ⁴Whoever says 'I know him' but does not keep his commandments is a liar, and the truth is not in him, ⁵but whoever keeps his word, in him truly the love of God is perfected. By this we may be sure that we are in him."*

So, how is it, according to the Bible—that *"we may be sure that we are in him?"* How may we know that we are indeed a Christian? Why, we are assured by acting in accordance with the Bible, by being in the ongoing process of sanctification, by demonstrating the existence of fruit in our lives.

Still, there are some (in fact, there are quite a few like William Cowper) who go through their life exhibiting doubt as to their position in Christ. And I am convinced that these are either people who suffer from some sort of internally caused clinical depression (like Cowper), or who are not fully dependent on the work of the Holy Spirit in their lives and are trying to strive on their own to live up to the Bible's requirements.

Remember what we said earlier about how futile it was to seek sanctification on our own. Even a man as brilliant as Ben Franklin failed. Recall that the process of sanctification is dependent on the work of the Holy Spirit in our lives. So it is with assurance of our salvation. Here's how it works. Not only are we to look at our lives to see the fruit of the Holy Spirit, to see the evidences of growth in sanctification, but also we must take into consideration the testimony of the Holy Spirit. In Romans 8:15-16, Paul writes, *"For you did not receive the spirit of slavery to fall back into fear, but you have received the Spirit of adoption as sons, by whom we cry, 'Abba! Father!'* [16]*The Spirit himself bears witness with our spirit that we are children of God."*

Not only are we allowed to see evidence of our truly being a Christian, the Holy Spirit himself *"bears witness"* that we are Christians. Ultimately, we are dependent on the work of the Holy Spirit in our lives to know we are saved. And so, if we don't know for sure that we are saved, then we must strive more and more to be filled with the Holy Spirit.

What happens if you are lacking in this filling of the Holy Spirit? One thing that might be true is that you just plain don't know—you totally lack assurance—but yet, you really are a believer. That was almost certainly the case of William Cowper. It was also the case of the author of Psalm 77. Notice these selected verses from the early part of that Psalm, written by a fellow much like Cowper, but he was named Asaph. Verse 2 reads, *"In the day of my trouble I seek the Lord; in the night my hand is stretched out without wearying; my soul refuses to be comforted."* Verse 4 tells, *"...I am so troubled that I cannot speak."* Verses 7-9 ask, *"Will the Lord spurn forever, and never again be favorable? Has his steadfast love forever ceased? Are his promises at an end for all time? Has God forgotten to be gracious? Has he in anger shut up his compassion?"*

Clearly, Asaph struggled with assurance. The only hope he had, he shared with us in verse 10, *"Then I said, 'I will appeal to this, to the years of the right hand of the Most High.'"* Asaph's only assurance came from examining his own life and seeing that, yes, he was faithful in the worship of God. It wasn't enough to keep him from struggling, but it was enough to offer some evidence. He went to church regularly. He was faithful at least in that.

But even those who are faithful in worship can sometimes have their assurance shaken. Certainly, King David of Israel was a faithful worshipper of God. But notice his lament, expressing how his assurance was shaken by the acknowledgement of sin in his life. From Psalm 51:8-12, *"Let me hear joy and gladness; let the bones that you have broken rejoice. [9]Hide your face from my sins, and blot out all my iniquities. [10]Create in me a clean heart, O God, and renew a right spirit within me. [11]Cast me not away from your presence, and take not your Holy Spirit from me. [12]Restore to me the joy of your salvation, and uphold me with a willing spirit."*

David's sins of adultery and of his being an accessory to murder had shaken the very foundations of his faith. There are others in the Bible like David. Peter's faith in Jesus was shaken when he denied his Savior three times on the night of Jesus' crucifixion. So, not every believer is guaranteed to have a strong assurance. But, we must at least be aware of the fact that the Bible teaches that *we should seek* it!

We are urged in 2 Peter 1:10, *"Therefore, brothers, be all the more diligent to make your calling and election sure, for if you practice these qualities you will never fall."* We are encouraged by Peter, who himself once was filled with doubts, to overcome our doubts and to be diligent to make our calling and election sure to ourselves. We do not lose our salvation by doubting, but we must remind ourselves, convince ourselves of our salvation so that we have the assurance, which makes us more useful in the kingdom. We are not responsible for becoming a Christian—but we are responsible for assuring ourselves that we are a Christian.

As I mentioned earlier, we are dependent on the work of the Holy Spirit in our lives to bear witness that we indeed are the children of God. But I must admit that this is a direct, spirit-to-spirit communication that cannot be analyzed, examined or explained. The broadly popular Christian writer J. I. Packer refers in his best selling book *Knowing God* to an old Scots woman who said of the work of the Holy Spirit, "It's more easily felt than tell't."

We don't know how we know—we just know. The sheep know the voice of the Shepherd. It's much like our sense of taste or sight. How does one know that the night is dark or that a lemon is sour? We just know. It is self-evident! God grants spiritual sense to his children. He makes it plain. He makes it obvious and real, and unmistakable to them. He gives us the confidence we need to feel secure, so when we feel insecure, we must go to him as King David did.

The fact that we can and should seek to have assurance, while at the same time understanding that our assurance will surely be shaken from time to time, is the balance of Scripture, and the balance desperately needed by the Church. Assurance is the birthright of the believer. The Christian religion, rightly understood, makes assurance possible. We ought to have assurance. We ought to seek it.

And we can be sure that God will give it, too! He will not withhold the security that we need and desire, but we must not expect it to come easily. Some have a harder time holding onto it than others do. Assurance is that certainty which comes in connection with a steady, consistent walk with the Lord. Assurance comes to those whose lives are being filled with the presence of the Holy Spirit. Without practicing these disciplines, you may not have assurance at all, but presumption. The saints, if they be saints (Christians), must and will persevere to the end and the Lord will see to it.

¹Now Jesus was praying in a certain place, and when he finished, one of his disciples said to him, "Lord, teach us to pray, as John taught his disciples." ²And he said to them, "When you pray, say: 'Father, hallowed be your name. Your kingdom come. ³Give us each day our daily bread, ⁴and forgive us our sins, for we ourselves forgive everyone who is indebted to us. And lead us not into temptation.' "

Luke 11:1-4

Chapter Nine
The Holy Spirit and Prayer

Most Christians who regularly recite what is known as The Lord's Prayer follow the version found in Matthew 6. When Luke recounts the same scene in chapter 11 of his gospel, the words are slightly different (which is quite typical of different accounts not only from the gospel writers, but from most people recounting something from memory).

I included the account from Luke's gospel because he recounts the question that leads up to the prayer. It's interesting to try to figure out why the different gospel writers include certain sayings of Jesus at different points in their gospels. Only Matthew records the entire Sermon on the Mount. Luke picks up pieces here and there, while Mark and John ignore it. I'm convinced it struck Matthew as extremely important because his entire gospel focuses more on Jesus' connection with the Old Testament than any of the other three.

But what's really interesting is to try to figure out why Luke repeats the Lord's Prayer long after the time period in his gospel of the Sermon on the Mount. We can't ever be sure of our answers to such questions, but I think my guess is a good one. I think Jesus first taught the model prayer during that long segment of teaching earlier on in his ministry, but by this time in Luke 11, the disciples had forgotten it.

Do you ever do that? Hear something in a sermon that sounds good, perhaps even important, and then forget it? Only later on, to try to remember what it was when a particular problem comes up?

The context of Luke 11 is just after Jesus had sent out 72 disciples (plus the inner circle of 12) to do mercy ministries in Samaria. My bet is some of them came back very discouraged, and somehow remembered that they were supposed to be praying as they went about doing their ministry. Thus the request in verse 1 of our text, *"Lord, teach us to pray."*

Every disciple of Jesus, every Christian, every one of you reading this who professes to be a Christian needs to learn how to pray. And I don't just mean you must memorize the Lord's Prayer so you can repeat it and use it. That is basic. That doesn't take much effort, even spiritually.

You and I face tough times and great struggles in our lives. We *really* need to learn everything we can about prayer—not just a kindergarten lesson. In fact, if we want to have powerful and effective prayer lives, if we really want to have God hear and answer our prayers, then we need to learn a lot more. And since our topic for this chapter is "The Holy Spirit and Prayer"—well then, we need to learn about prayer *in* the Holy Spirit, prayer *by* the Holy Spirit, prayer *to* the Holy Spirit and prayer *for* the Holy Spirit.

If there was ever one essential biblical rule for how a Christian is to pray, it is that they must pray *in* the

Holy Spirit! That exact phrase *"pray in the Spirit"* is used specifically at least twice in the New Testament, in Ephesians 6:18 and Jude 1:20. However, an Old Testament passage is most helpful in understanding what it means. That is in Zechariah 12:10. *"And I will pour out on the house of David and the inhabitants of Jerusalem a spirit of grace and pleas for mercy, so that, when they look on me, on him whom they have pierced, they shall mourn for him, as one mourns for an only child, and weep bitterly over him, as one weeps over a firstborn."*

Zechariah was predicting the pouring out of the Spirit upon all Christians at Pentecost, 40 days after Jesus ascended into heaven. (We'll look at that in depth in a later chapter.) In the NIV and King James translations of that verse, the Holy Spirit is called *"the Spirit of grace and supplication."* "Supplication" means asking and requesting, and is a special term for prayer. The ESV translation of "pleas for mercy" is even better.

So then, Zechariah's prophecy foretold that God would pour out at Pentecost the Spirit of prayer when he poured out the Holy Spirit. To say that Christians have the Spirit of prayer in their lives is essentially the same as saying that they pray in the Spirit.

So what does that mean in a practical sense? Well, it means that without the Holy Spirit, true prayer, prayer that reaches the ears of God the Father, is impossible. Without faith in Jesus, prayer lacks the proper motive to make it pleasing to God. This means that you must be regenerated by the Holy Spirit, and in the process of being sanctified through the indwelling work of the Holy Spirit, if you want your prayers to be *in* the Holy Spirit.

Another practical working out of prayer in the Spirit is that even if we are not sure what to pray for, the Holy Spirit will make sure we get it right. Paul writes in Romans 8:26, *"Likewise the Spirit helps us in our weakness. For we do not know what to pray for as we ought, but the Spirit himself intercedes for us with groanings too deep for words."*

Sometimes you and I are confronted with choices and we don't know which one is the best for us, or more importantly, which one is the one God wants for us. Sometimes we are confronted with problems or worries that are impossible for us to get out of on our own. At times, we do not even understand the scriptural principles that apply to these issues.

So, if we are to have a fruitful prayer life, we must trust that the Holy Spirit will do one of two things. Either he will show us in the Scriptures what is best and therefore what to pray for or he will pray for the correct choice himself. Either way, we are praying in the Spirit.

Praying in the Spirit also means that the Spirit will give us the confidence that God is going to hear and answer our prayers. It works the same way that our assurance of salvation works, which was discussed in the previous chapter. John writes in his famous letter on assurance, in 1 John 5:14, *"And this is the confidence that we have toward him, that if we ask anything according to his will he hears us."*

In the same way, someone may actually be a Christian even though they do not have assurance; God will answer a Christian's prayers even if they are not sure that he is hearing them. We don't have to depend on our own ability to pray. We don't have to learn a lot of fancy words and phrases to use in our prayers. We simply need to allow the Holy Spirit dwelling in us to assist us to pray *in* the Spirit.

Let's move on to the second concept we need to learn about prayer—that of prayer *by* the Holy Spirit. Looking again at Romans 8, this time reading both verses 26 and 27, we see, *"Likewise the Spirit helps us in our weakness. For we do not know what to pray for as we ought, but the Spirit himself intercedes for us with groanings too deep for words. [27]And he who searches hearts knows what is the mind of the Spirit, because the Spirit intercedes for the saints according to the will of God."* The fact is that just as the Holy Spirit is responsible for our regeneration, and our sanctification, and for granting us assurance, he is also responsible for our prayers. So, if there is some reason that we are unable to pray rightly to God, the Holy Spirit will do it in our behalf.

What a great comfort that is to Christians. Not only is God the Son, Jesus, standing at the right hand of God, next to the very throne of grace, praying in our behalf. But, at the same time, God the Holy Spirit is here on earth dwelling in our hearts, interceding for us in matters that we may not even be aware of at all.

Have you ever received a totally unexpected blessing in your life that came without any knowledge to you, and especially came without any prayer on your part? I believe every spiritually minded Christian has noticed a number of experiences like that. I know I have. Something you didn't even know you needed, or wanted—and most likely something you didn't deserve—God just gave it to you. Now you know why that happened ... because the Holy Spirit asked God in your behalf! There really is a great blessing to Christians from the work of prayer *by* the Holy Spirit whether we are aware of it or not.

Next, let's think about prayer *to* the Holy Spirit. Sometimes people ask the question "Is it proper to pray *to* the Spirit? Aren't we supposed to pray to the Father, and in the name of the Son?" Even within Bible-believing Presbyterian circles, there are differences of opinion on this issue. The question is, "When we pray to God, must it be addressed only to the single person of God the Father, as separate from God the Son and God the Holy Spirit?"

If you take time to carefully review the material in the Bible that relates to this question—and I'm not going to take time in this short book to rehearse all of that with you—you will find that all indications are that prayer is indeed normally intended for the Father, for the first person of the Trinity. That is why most Christians start out their prayers with the word "Father" somewhere in the very first phrase. Jesus even encouraged his followers to pray in his name, but directed to his Father. We find that recorded in John 15:16. *"You did not choose me, but I chose you and appointed you that you should go and bear fruit and that your fruit should abide, so that whatever you ask the Father in my name, he may give it to you."*

I think it is striking that Jesus himself did not pray directly to the Holy Spirit. Even when he was praying for the Holy Spirit to come to comfort his followers after he would leave them, he prayed to the Father and not directly to the Holy Spirit (John 14:16).

When you read all of Paul's epistles, you see over and over again that he prays almost exclusively to *"the God and Father of our Lord Jesus Christ,"* which is to say to the first person of the Trinity. So I think we can rightly conclude that the Bible teaches us that we are to direct our prayers chiefly to the God the Father.

However, it is possible there will be times in which it is proper and even desirable to pray to each person of the Trinity—to Jesus, and even to the Holy Spirit. Because they sustain special relationships to us and have done special things for us, we at times may go to them individually—with this important warning: while there is no biblical evidence instructing us *not* to do so, we must be very careful not to abuse this freedom. Putting too much stress on prayer either to Jesus or to the Holy Spirit misses the clear emphasis about prayer to the Father. I'm afraid there are a number of Christians today who are abusing that freedom with their almost exclusive focus on prayers to the Holy Spirit.

Let me give you some examples of how praying to the Spirit might be appropriate at times. We should be praying to the Father when we have need for his love, and his care, and his protection—all the issues involving his daily providence in our lives that he promises. But we may pray directly to Jesus when we desire to be forgiven for our sins and washed of them. After all, it was Jesus who died to remove the guilt and stain of our sins.

In the same way, it is permissible to pray to the Holy Spirit. If you were suffering with great grief and bereavement, it would be a great blessing to pray directly to the Holy Spirit. After all, the Spirit is the Spirit of comfort. He is the one whose task it is to console us. Or perhaps you notice there is a lack of sanctification in your life; you are not dealing with your sins the way you know you should; you are not growing in your relationship to God. Well, it would be proper to pray to the Spirit to continue to make you holy, for that is one of his prime works in our lives. The same could be said of praying to the Spirit for assurance. That, too, is his work. So, yes, we may pray directly to the Holy Spirit. In fact, in the hymnals designed for Presbyterian congregations, you will find a number of wonderful hymns directed to the Holy Spirit.

Finally, we want to consider our fourth point about the Holy Spirit and prayer. Not only should we have prayer *in* the Spirit, and *by* the Spirit, and *to* the Spirit.

We must also pray *for* the Spirit. In this book, we have been learning a lot about the work of the Holy Spirit in our lives. I hope by this point, we are all now more aware of what the Holy Spirit is doing in us and through us. So it should be clear that we don't just need to have more information, we also need to have more spiritual activity.

In Chapter Ten, we will look specifically at the issue of the fullness of the Holy Spirit, the direct correlation between spiritual strength and being Spirit-filled. So, it should almost go without saying, you and I need to be praying *for* the Spirit to work in us more and more, bringing us to a greater level of sanctification, helping us deal with sin in our lives, bringing a deeper level of assurance, bringing more joy and peace to our lives.

The same thing is true of prayer itself. If our prayer life is dull, drab, burdensome or not enjoyable; if we hardly bother to pray or feel out of touch with God as if our prayers do not reach him; if we do not know what to pray for and prayer is not a means of power and grace in our lives, then we can go to the Spirit of prayer himself and ask him to come into our lives more fully in this area of weakness.

[12]For just as the body is one and has many members, and all the members of the body, though many, are one body, so it is with Christ. [13]For in one Spirit we were all baptized into one body—Jews or Greeks, slaves or free—and all were made to drink of one Spirit. [14]For the body does not consist of one member but of many.

1 Corinthians 12:12-14

[29]The next day he saw Jesus coming toward him, and said, "Behold, the Lamb of God, who takes away the sin of the world! [30]This is he of whom I said, 'After me comes a man who ranks before me, because he was before me.' [31]I myself did not know him, but for this purpose I came baptizing with water, that he might be revealed to Israel." [32]And John bore witness: "I saw the Spirit descend from heaven like a dove, and it remained on him. [33]I myself did not know him, but he who sent me to baptize with water said to me, 'He on whom you see the Spirit descend and remain, this is he who baptizes with the Holy Spirit.' "

John 1:29-33

Chapter Ten
The Baptism and Fullness of the Holy Spirit

I n this chapter and the next, we will be dealing with the heart of the controversy in our age between churches and individuals today who believe that miraculous gifts are normative or regularly expected, and those who do not. Those churches that do believe they are to be regularly expected are generally referred to as Charismatic or Pentecostal. Because of the widespread nature of this controversy, let me set a few ground rules for these two chapters.

Ground rule number one: In these chapters, we will examine *only* what the Bible says. This should go without saying, but it is necessary to say it when it comes to this topic. We will not discuss the *experiences* of any particular people or groups.

Ground rule number two: We will *not* discuss all the possible issues in these two chapters. Rather we will cover the more positive, basic issues taught in the Bible.

Ground rule number three: As we seek to study the Bible on this issue, we must differentiate between places in the Bible where the teaching is didactic (where the Bible intends to teach us something) and places where the Bible merely gives historical examples or stories.

Think, for instance, about the story of Philemon and his runaway slave, Onesimus. You may recall that in his letter to Philemon, Paul dealt with principles of how Christians should deal with each other—no matter our station in life. Those principles apply to all of us. But in the historical setting of that story, the bible speaks of the existence of slavery. Just because the Bible mentions the existence of slavery does *not mean* that the Bible approves of slavery. That is not at all what Paul was trying to get across.

So, you and I must always learn to separate the didactic, normative teaching of the Bible from the historical examples contained in the Bible. The examples are not necessarily there to teach us anything.

OK, let's get down to business. Our topic in the next chapter will be the *gifts* of the Spirit. Our first topic is the baptism and fullness of the Spirit. What is it that the Bible clearly, unambiguously teaches about the baptism and fullness of the Holy Spirit?

We want to start with 1 Corinthians 12:12-14. This text follows Paul's extensive teaching about the gifts of the Spirit (we'll talk about them later). But after discussing the gifts of the Spirit, Paul reminds us of what had previously been taught in the New Testament, even by Jesus himself. *"For just as the body is one and has many members, and all the members of the body, though many, are one body, so it is with Christ. ¹³For in one Spirit we were all baptized into one body—Jews or Greeks, slaves or free—and all were made to drink of one Spirit. ¹⁴For the body does not consist of one member but of many."*

While it was certainly Paul's intention to teach most specifically about the issue that Christians are all part of one body, the Church, he uses baptism as an illustration, in fact as a simile, to present another important truth. It is verse 13, *"For in one Spirit we were all baptized into one body—Jews or Greeks, slaves or free—and all were made to drink of one Spirit."* Pretty clear, isn't it? Everyone in the body of Christ, which is to say everyone in the Church, which is to say *every Christian*, has been baptized in the Spirit and made to drink of one spirit.

Let me repeat that in slightly different words. Every Christian has been baptized with the Holy Spirit at the time he or she received Christ as Savior. Thus, every Christian must be drinking in the Holy Spirit, be full of the Holy Spirit. These are the two halves of this chapter. The baptism of the Holy Spirit is for everyone—not for a special few—and every Christian has the Holy Spirit within himself. John the Baptizer promised that would happen when he said, as reported in Mark 1:8, *"I have baptized you with water, but he will baptize you with the Holy Spirit."* Of course, the "he" in that verse is Jesus. It is our Savior himself, who brings us the baptism of the Holy Spirit.

If that's not enough to convince you, look at the Apostle John's account. The entire first chapter of his gospel gives us details of John the Baptizer's explanation of the work of Jesus. Here's the summary, contained in John 1:29-33. *"The next day he saw Jesus coming toward him, and said, 'Behold, the Lamb of God, who takes away the sin of the world! [30]This is he of whom I said, "After me comes a man who ranks before me, because he was before me."[31]I myself did not know him, but for this purpose I came baptizing with water, that he might be revealed to Israel.' [32]And John bore witness: 'I saw the Spirit descend from heaven like a dove, and it remained on him. [33]I myself did not know him, but he who sent me to baptize with water said to me, "He on whom you see the Spirit descend and remain, this is he who baptizes with the Holy Spirit." '"*

Once again we see the same thing there in verse 33, Jesus baptizes with the Holy Spirit. But what else does Jesus do? Back in verse 29, John says *"Behold, the Lamb of God, who takes away the sin of the world!"* These are the two great things that happen in the life of every single person who becomes a Christian. Jesus takes away our sins and Jesus gives us the Holy Spirit. They happen at the same time; you can't have one without the other. If you have the Holy Spirit in your life, then you are regenerated—born again—and you are in the process of being sanctified, having your sins dealt with. Or to put it in the opposite terms, if you do not have the Holy Spirit, then your sins are not forgiven; you are dead in sin.

Either you are a Christian who have had your sins washed away and have received the Holy Spirit (or to use John the Baptizer's terminology, have been baptized in the Holy Spirit), *or,* you are not a Christian. The baptism with water is a sign of either the presumption (in adults) of the baptism of the Holy Spirit or (in children) of the promise of the work of the Holy Spirit. That is why the Christian Church has *always* used the Sacrament of Baptism as a sign of admission to the Church. Some churches believe the Sacrament of Baptism is the very time when a person is baptized with the Holy Spirit, but even in their theological error, they still recognize the connection between becoming a Christian and being baptized with the Holy Spirit.

OK, that's the first half of what we need to learn on this topic, every Christian has received the baptism of the Holy Spirit. Now we must learn the second half, the issue about the fullness of the Holy Spirit. One of the biggest problems in the life of many Christians is that they somehow think that once they become a Christian (once they have been baptized with the Holy Spirit) they can go about living their lives any way they like. Do you remember our discussion of the heresy of the Carnal Christian two chapters earlier?

That is not what happens. Anyone who becomes a Christian *will* be in the process of sanctification; they *will* be in the process of dealing with and overcoming sin in their lives. We made it quite clear that it takes the ongoing work of the Holy Spirit to do that. And the only way you can be successful at that process of sanctification is if you are *filled* with the Holy Spirit. The measure is important—the more *full* you are, the more sanctified you will be.

Does that sound a lot like a Holiness Church teaching to you? Well, let's give credit where credit is due, that part of it they got exactly right. Let's review a litany of biblical passages in the Old and New Testaments that teach exactly that point—that believers are to be filled with the Spirit. Exodus 31:3 speaks of the artisans who built the tabernacle in the wilderness. *"And I have filled him* [them] *with the Spirit of God, with ability and intelligence, with knowledge and all craftsmanship."* Ezekiel 37:1 relates, *"The hand of the Lord was upon me, and he brought me out in the Spirit of the Lord and set me down in the middle of the valley; it was full of bones."*

Micah 3:8 testifies, *"But as for me, I am filled with power, with the Spirit of the LORD, and with justice and might..."* In Luke 1:15, the angel speaking of the uniqueness of John the Baptizer as a baby says, *"For he will be great before the Lord. And he must not drink wine or strong drink, and he will be filled with the Holy Spirit, even from his mother's womb."* Peter also had it. *"Then Peter, filled with the Holy Spirit, said to them…"* (Acts 4:8)

Acts 4:31 tells us, *"And when they had prayed, the place in which they were gathered together was shaken, and they were all filled with the Holy Spirit and continued to speak the word of God with boldness."* Acts 9:17 describes the conversion of Paul. *"So Ananias departed and entered the house. And laying his hands on him he said, 'Brother Saul, the Lord Jesus who appeared to you on the road by which you came has sent me so that you may regain your sight and be filled with the Holy Spirit.'"*

In Acts 13:52, it is pictured. *"And the disciples were filled with joy and with the Holy Spirit."* As it was in Ephesians 5:18, *"And do not get drunk with wine, for that is debauchery, but be filled with the Spirit."*

Actually, we have only scratched the surface, but I think it should be clear that God provides the fullness of the Holy Spirit. He desires that each of us be so filled that we can use our gifts in service to God. Surely, that is what Jesus meant in that unique incident described in John 7:37-39. The background is the Feast of Tabernacles. Jesus and his followers had come to Jerusalem to celebrate this important Jewish holiday. The Feast of Tabernacles was a weeklong celebration of how God had provided for the Jewish people during their 40 years of wandering in the wilderness. During the feast, celebrants would themselves actually live in tents. And the best location to pitch a tent was in the courtyards of the Temple.

One of the special ceremonies during the Feast of Tabernacles was the ceremonial pouring out of water from a huge pitcher—as a symbol of how God provided water to assuage the Jews' thirst in the desert. Well, this particular year, Jesus made his own point about this ceremony. *"On the last day of the feast, the great day, Jesus stood up and cried out, 'If anyone thirsts, let him come to me and drink.* [38]*Whoever believes in me, as the Scripture has said, "Out of his heart will flow rivers of living water."'* [39]*Now this he said about the Spirit, whom those who believed in him were to receive..."*

Clearly, Jesus uses the pouring of water to symbolize receiving the baptism of the Holy Spirit—as all of his believers would receive at Pentecost. But notice that phrase in verse 38, *"Out of his heart will flow rivers of living water."* Tell me please, how is it that *"rivers of living water"* can flow *out* of a believer's heart? Isn't it obvious? This word picture symbolizes the Holy Spirit and their hearts must be full for such a volume to pour out. It is only when we are *filled* with the Holy Spirit that we can use our spiritual gifts to bring glory to God and to serve others.

If you want to be involved in sharing the good news of the gospel with others, your own heart must be full of the Holy Spirit. If you want to provide mercy to those in need in the name of Jesus, your heart must be full of the Holy Spirit. If you want to use your gifts of preaching, or teaching, or leadership, or stewardship—you must be full of the Holy Spirit.

Now, one final question remains to be answered about the fullness of the Holy Spirit. And that is "How do I get full?" When you think about it, the question is "How do I receive *any* amount of the Holy Spirit?" You see, fullness is simply a function of using whatever means are available to us to the proper extent that we can become full. I hope you have been taught this before. What are the ways by which you and I can receive more and more of the Holy Spirit—so that we might be filled? It is by those things that we call the means of grace. And what are they? Basically, there are three: the Bible, prayer and the Sacraments.

When you hear the Bible preached—and especially when you read the Bible on your own—you are in the process of being filled with the Holy Spirit. When you pray—whether in church, or a small prayer group—but especially when you pray daily on your own in your quiet time with God—you are in the process of being filled with the Holy Spirit. And when you participate in the Sacraments—especially those wonderful worship services when we come to the table of the Lord to celebrate the Lord's Supper—you are in the process of being filled with the Holy Spirit.

So, think about this. Most of our day-to-day life is spent using up whatever measure of the Holy Spirit we have, dealing in relationships, performing in our vocations, participating in recreation. Most of our time is spent using up whatever measure of the Holy Spirit's strength we might have in reserve. So, if we start out a day without "filling up" our reserves through our own prayer and Bible reading, what kind of day might we expect to have? If we start out our week without "filling up" our reserves through gathering in worship with our brothers and sisters in the Lord— what kind of week might we expect to have?

Anytime you come home and say, "Boy, I had a terrible day"—ask yourself if the reason might have been that you did not fill up with the Holy Spirit that day. Anytime you see someone at church, and they ask you how things are going and you are tempted to say, "Boy, did I ever have one of those weeks," ask yourself if you have been failing to utilize all the opportunities you have to fill up through the means of grace.

I'm not saying that life will be perfect this side of heaven. But what I am saying and what the Bible is teaching us is that without the fullness of the Holy Spirit we can never expect to have the spiritual strength to deal with others. Or, to serve others, to minister to others, and certainly, we can never expect to have the spiritual strength to share the good news of the gospel with others.

Yes, it is God's work to bring us to the point in our lives where we can be sure that we have received the Baptism of the Holy Spirit, to say that we are sure that we are Christians. But it is our work to ensure that we, on a regular, daily basis, are in the process of being filled with the Spirit. Oh, have no doubt, God provides the means and does the actual work of filling us up but we must avail ourselves of those means. Running water from a faucet is of no help to a man dying of thirst if he doesn't drink it. The means of grace by which you and I can be filled with the Holy Spirit are of no help to a person suffering from spiritual thirst, if he doesn't use those means to be filled.

If you are a Christian, if you have been baptized with the Holy Spirit, then you *will* do two things: Use the means of grace! Be filled with the Holy Spirit!

¹Now concerning spiritual gifts, brothers, I do not want you to be uninformed. ²You know that when you were pagans you were led astray to mute idols, however you were led. ³Therefore I want you to understand that no one speaking in the Spirit of God ever says "Jesus is accursed!" and no one can say "Jesus is Lord" except in the Holy Spirit. ⁴Now there are varieties of gifts, but the same Spirit; ⁵and there are varieties of service, but the same Lord; ⁶and there are varieties of activities, but it is the same God who empowers them all in everyone.

1 Corinthians 12:1-6

Chapter Eleven
The Gifts of the Holy Spirit

As we begin this chapter, please notice the plural word in the title—gifts. There is a difference between the singular and plural form of this word when used in relationship to the Holy Spirit. The "gift" (singular) of the Holy Spirit was our topic in the last chapter on the baptism of the Spirit. Every, single, solitary Christian receives the Holy Spirit at conversion—this is the gift that God gives to us.

In addition to this singular gift, every single, solitary Christian also receives something else from God. This we call the "gifts" of the Spirit, which is the topic of this chapter. In addition, each person receives different gifts; no two Christians are exactly alike in what gifts they have or don't have, and to what capacity they have the various gifts.

In the Bible, there are four lists of the various spiritual gifts. Appendix A contains a listing that shows you those gifts and the various English words used to translate the Greek words. We have to pick one of these four lists to start, and just about every commentator on this topic starts with the list in 1 Corinthians 12:1-6. *"Now concerning spiritual gifts, brothers, I do not want you to be uninformed. ²You know that when you were pagans you were led astray to mute idols, however you were led. ³Therefore I want you to understand that no one speaking in the Spirit of God ever says 'Jesus is accursed!' and no one can say 'Jesus is Lord' except in the Holy Spirit. [4]Now there are varieties of gifts, but the same Spirit; [5]and there are varieties of service, but the same Lord; [6]and there are varieties of activities, but it is the same God who empowers them all in everyone."*

Looking especially at verses 4 through 6, notice that there is only one giver of these gifts, one Spirit, one Lord, one God. All Spiritual gifts come from God. In these verses, there are three separate words used describing the same concept. In verse 4, the Greek word *charismata* is used (looks like charismatic, right?), which is translated as "gifts." Then in verse 5, the Greek word *diakoinia* is used (looks like deacon, right?), which is translated as "service." Finally in verse 6, the Greek word *energemata* is used (looks like energy, right?), which is translated as "activity," or "energy," or "power."

So with this background we are ready to define the key term we need to understand. Just what is a spiritual gift? Well, a spiritual gift is a certain capacity, bestowed by God's grace and power, which fits people for specific and corresponding service. For instance, each Christian gets something special to do in the Church. Not everyone has the same calling, the same area of service. Further, each person is given one or more corresponding spiritual gifts to match that calling. The best way to know what God wants you to be doing in the Church (in other words, the best way to determine your calling or service for God) should be to determine what your spiritual gifts are.

Now, in a small church, you frequently have people volunteering for a service who are not especially gifted for that job. That is because within a small group of people you frequently do not find all the spiritual gifts needed for all the things people want to see happening in a church. Playing musical instruments is a good illustration for most churches. Some have to use electronic means, such as a digital hymnal to play music for hymns, because God has not gifted anyone in the fellowship to have the kind of ability and repertoire to play so many different songs.

The next issue to look at is the number of different spiritual gifts. Lot's of people hear the words "spiritual gifts" and think immediately of the "big three"—tongues, prophesy and healing. But there are many, many more, and frankly, many that are far more important today. You can see from the list in Appendix A that there are at least twenty-one, perhaps more. 1 Corinthians 12 lists thirteen; Romans 12 gives five different ones; Ephesians 4 names two additional ones and 1 Peter 4 specifies one new gift. The thing is … these lists (just like most lists in the Bible) are not necessarily meant to be exhaustive.

So, in verse 6 we see that everyone has a spiritual gift, and we know that spiritual gifts are given by God to equip people for service to him. We know there are a lot of different gifts—more than 20 for sure. None of that is very controversial, is it? The controversy comes when you look at these lists and you notice that some of them involve the performing of miracles and some don't. Gifts like wisdom (1 Corinthians 12:8) and serving (mentioned both in Romans 12 and in 1 Peter 4) are obviously very mundane, ordinary, non-miraculous gifts. However, 1 Corinthians 12 contains a number that clearly require the performing of miracles—healing, tongues and such.

A big part of the problem in churches today is that many people think only of the miraculous gifts when they speak of spiritual gifts. That is wrong. The term Charismatic gifts (to use the Greek word for them) refers to all spiritual gifts—not just the miraculous ones. However, the issue of miraculous gifts is what causes all the controversy today. So, we need to spend a little time considering this issue.

To begin with, you and I need to have a balanced view of miracles. You see, miracles are not impossible today. A miracle, by definition, is God intervening in the natural order of the universe to do something supernatural. He can and will do whatever he wants, whenever he wants. Sometimes we speak of the birth of a baby as a miracle. Technically, that is not correct. The birth of a baby follows the normal course of the human condition. As glorious and wonderful as a birth is, it is not a miracle. But when Jesus was born of a virgin, without the normal course of human conception that was a miracle. God had to intervene supernaturally.

Another illustration is that of healing. Sometimes we speak of someone recovering from a disease like cancer as a miracle. My wife has overcome breast cancer and, at the time of this writing, has been diagnosed as cancer-free after eight months of treatment for ovarian cancer. We refer to all that as a miracle. However, most of the time (although we may not understand how it all works) those recoveries are part of the normal course of the human condition. I believe it is very rare that God supernaturally intervenes to bring about a cure. In the area of cancer research, there is much still to learn about what is going on naturally. But—when someone is raised from the ultimate disease condition of death—then *that* is a miracle; *that* is God's supernatural intervention.

So, by definition, miracles are *not* normative; they don't normally occur. If they were normal, everyday, commonplace, they would be part of the usual condition and they would therefore not be miracles.

It is not a gift given to many. Even many great biblical characters did not perform miracles. We are told in John 10:41 that John the Baptist did not perform any miracles, yet Jesus refers to him as the greatest of all the Old Testament prophets. In the same way, the miraculous charismatic gifts are not normative today.

When you examine carefully the role of miracles in the Bible, you see that they occur at four different, main periods of biblical history, providing evidence that the authors of Scripture were writing and speaking God's word. Miracles were seen in the time of Moses—in the giving of the Law. They occurred in the days of Elijah, Elisha and others—in the giving of the books known as the Prophets. They happened all around Jesus—in the giving of the Gospels. And they took place in the days of the Apostles—in the giving of the Epistles. The major purpose of miracles in the Bible was to authenticate each fresh, new stage of God's revelation to man, which when written down and preserved, became what we know as the Bible. In short, miracles confirmed that God's revelation was true.

Now, we have learned many times before that the Bible, God's revelation to man, is the only authority in our lives and in the Church. One of the great principles of the Reformation was *Sola Scriptura*—the Scriptures alone, meaning that no traditions or opinions of men, only the Bible, can be looked to as trustworthy. In addition, we know that the Bible, God's revelation to man, is finished. It is complete. There are to be no new direct revelations from God.

This is a central issue, which separates churches holding to the original principles of the Reformation from others. Many groups today do not believe what Reformation-based churches believe. Mormons, Christian Scientists, Roman Catholics, and many (but not all) Charismatics and Pentecostals all believe that there *is* new revelation that comes from God today—in addition to the Bible.

One application of this truth is that every Christian needs to get that issue settled in their minds. Either there *is* new revelation from God, or there *isn't*. It is important that you know what you believe in that regard. Otherwise, if you think one way and are in a church that believes and teaches the other way, you will never be happy. Reformation-based churches (such as my denomination, the Presbyterian Church in America) believe revelation is closed—and if you believe in new revelation, you'll never be satisfied in churches like that.

The other main application of this issue of completed revelation is that we are never to expect a new cluster of miracles, which would confirm a new revelation. Thus, we are not to expect a return of the miraculous Charismatic gifts. Since miraculous gifts— including tongues, prophecy and healing—were part and parcel of the authentication of revelation and there is no longer any new revelation, we should not expect to see these miraculous gifts today.

Does that mean that they never occur? Of course not. God can bring about a miracle any time he wants to. Occasionally you hear of a missionary coming back from working from a people group that had never had their language put into writing, and thus had never read the Bible. Once in a while, you see a miraculous gift or two occur in these settings to help this new people group understand the authentication of the Bible.

But for you and me living in America in the 21st Century, that is not the case. Until recent years, it was rare to run into anyone in the United States who had never heard about Jesus, or was unaware that the Bible is purported to be the word of God. Non-Christians may not have believed it, but they at least knew the essentials. In fact, one of the main tenants of the Reformation is that everything you and I need to know about God and about life, as God wants us to live it, is already in the Bible. We don't need any new revelation. And thus, we don't need any miraculous gifts.

This is the overwhelming clear statement of the doctrinal standards of Bible-believing Presbyterian churches—the Westminster Confession of Faith. The following is from Section 1-4.

> "The whole counsel of God concerning all things necessary for his own glory, man's salvation, faith and life, is either expressly set down in Scripture, or by good and necessary consequence may be deduced from Scripture; unto which nothing at any time is to be added, whether by new revelations of the Spirit or traditions of men."

Even more importantly, when you look at the Bible you see the "whole counsel" in many different contexts. When you look at the training and gifting of the apostles, you see that it was Jesus' intention to close the canon (and all revelation) through them. Examine these extracts from the gospels. Mark 3:13-15 reads, *"And he went up on the mountain and called to him those whom he desired, and they came to him. ¹⁴And he appointed twelve (whom he also named apostles) so that they might be with him and he might send them out to preach ¹⁵and have authority to cast out demons."* John 13:30-31 tells us, *"So, after receiving the morsel of bread, he [Judas] immediately went out. And it was night. ³¹When he had gone out, Jesus said, 'Now is the Son of Man glorified, and God is glorified in him.' "* Notice that Judas is identified and then leaves. This Upper Room teaching (Jesus is glorified and God is glorified in him) is intended only for the real disciples of Jesus. Then we read John 14:26, *"But the Helper, the Holy Spirit, whom the Father will send in my name, he will teach you all things and bring to your remembrance all that I have said to you."* Here we see that the Holy Spirit will teach them what they need to know. This is a special promise for the apostles.

A bit further in the gospel, in John 15:15, we read, *"No longer do I call you servants, for the servant does not know what his master is doing; but I have called you friends, for all that I have heard from my Father I have made known to you."* Only the apostles receive the ability to remember everything Jesus taught them so they could record it in the Bible.

Finally in John 20:21 we see, *"Jesus said to them again, 'Peace be with you. As the Father has sent me, even so I am sending you.' "* Here we see that the apostles understood they had a special calling from Jesus that none of the other thousands of followers had received. Clearly, when the apostles wrote Scripture, they showed that they understood the principles Jesus had taught them, that what they were to write down were all things that they had been taught.

Other parts of the Bible support the same proposition. Rev 22:18 cautions, *"I warn everyone who hears the words of the prophecy of this book: if anyone adds to them, God will add to him the plagues described in this book."* Here we see that no new teachings are to be added to the Bible. Jude 1:3 reads, *"Beloved, although I was very eager to write to you about our common salvation, I found it necessary to write appealing to you to contend for the faith that was once for all delivered to the saints."* The truths of the faith (the Bible) were *"once for all delivered." And* 2 Timothy 1:13-14 qualifies, *"Follow the pattern of the sound words that you have heard from me, in the faith and love that are in Christ Jesus. ¹⁴By the Holy Spirit who dwells within us, guard the good deposit entrusted to you."* Scripture is called a *"good deposit."* No additional deposits are needed.

With the understanding that what the apostles did was unique and very special, and required the authentication of miraculous gifts, we are ready to understand that not all of the spiritual gifts we see in the Bible are given today. The gifts given to the apostles,

Prophets (and Evangelists, if understood as "Apostolic Helpers" as discussed at length in my book *Biblical Church Government*) do not exist today. These men were designated individuals with certain gifts and training for their specific missions. The miraculous gifts for the purpose of revelation (tongues, interpretation, healing, miracles, etc.) do not exist today because their purpose has ceased.

Be encouraged to know that, on the list of charismatic gifts that follows in Appendix A, while there are a few that are not in effect today, there are still plenty to go around, and the Church needs people who have and who use these gifts on a regular basis. In Appendix B, there is an outline of the examination of the one, miraculous, charismatic gift that is at the center of controversy today—speaking in tongues.

In the meantime, if God ensures that the things he wants to happen in the Church get done because he gives people spiritual gifts to do them, then you and I better be sure that we know what our gifts are. Then we'd better put them to use in a way that both supports the Church *and especially* brings honor and glory to Jesus.

¹Now there was a man of the Pharisees named Nicodemus, a ruler of the Jews. ²This man came to Jesus by night and said to him, "Rabbi, we know that you are a teacher come from God, for no one can do these signs that you do unless God is with him." ³Jesus answered him, "Truly, truly, I say to you, unless one is born again he cannot see the kingdom of God." ⁴Nicodemus said to him, "How can a man be born when he is old? Can he enter a second time into his mother's womb and be born?" ⁵Jesus answered, "Truly, truly, I say to you, unless one is born of water and the Spirit, he cannot enter the kingdom of God. ⁶That which is born of the flesh is flesh, and that which is born of the Spirit is spirit. ⁷Do not marvel that I said to you, 'You must be born again.' ⁸The wind blows where it wishes, and you hear its sound, but you do not know where it comes from or where it goes. So it is with everyone who is born of the Spirit." ⁹Nicodemus said to him, "How can these things be?" ¹⁰Jesus answered him, "Are you the teacher of Israel and yet you do not understand these things? ¹¹Truly, truly, I say to you, we speak of what we know, and bear witness to what we have seen, but you do not receive our testimony. ¹²If I have told you earthly things and you do not believe, how can you believe if I tell you heavenly things? ¹³No one has ascended into heaven except him who descended from heaven, the Son of Man. ¹⁴And as Moses lifted up the serpent in the wilderness, so must the Son of Man be lifted up, ¹⁵that whoever believes in him may have eternal life."

John 3:1-15

Chapter Twelve
Symbols of the Holy Spirit in the Bible

E asy to understand (some would call them down-to-earth) illustrations are very helpful to someone learning about a new subject. If you read the first eleven chapters of this book, you have seen a few of those illustrations. In this final chapter, we want to look at a whole series of illustrations found in the Bible that were designed by Jesus and the apostolic writers to help people understand the concept of the Holy Spirit.

Lots of illustrations are used in the Bible, especially in the New Testament. Jesus compared himself to a door, a street, a piece of bread and a cup of water. For illustrations about the kingdom of God, he compared it to a pearl, a fish net, a supper, a tree, a seed and a hidden treasure. Paul also could illustrate deep theological issues. He used references to stars, the foundation of a house, the parts of a body, light and darkness, hay and pearls.

There are a number of illustrations in the Bible that are intended to help us better understand the person and work of the Holy Spirit. We have already learned that the Spirit, although he is a person, is invisible, and as part of the Triune God, is ultimately incomprehensible. Just thinking about those attributes makes it very hard for someone to get a handle on just who the Holy Spirit is and what he is doing.

The good news is that God understands our human limitations and has given us in the Bible symbols about the Holy Spirit, visible signs to help us understand an invisible reality. The Bible compares the Holy Spirit to water, wind, breath, fire, oil, a dove, a fruit tree, a down payment and a seal. By looking at and trying to understand some of these symbols, it is possible to come to a greater insight into the many aspects of the work of the Holy Spirit.

Let's begin with *water*. In several places, the Bible closely associates the Holy Spirit with water. There really are two reasons for this. One, it indicates that the Holy Spirit cleanses the inner self the way water cleanses the outer self. And two, water indicates that the Holy Spirit is the source of life, just the way a person, animal or plant must have water to live.

Most children would understand both of these aspects of the symbol of water. We know all too well how children can play outside and get muddy. Children, whether on purpose or not, can smear mud on their pants, on their faces and in their hair. However, we know that there is one main remedy for dirt—water! It will remove the mud from their clothes, face and hair, so that all that was dirty will be sparkling clean again (for a while, at least).

This is the imagery the Bible uses of the regenerating work of the Holy Spirit. It shows man as being figuratively dirty, filthy and polluted because of his sin but when the Holy Spirit comes into a person's life, it cleanses that person from his sin. He regenerates the heart and sanctifies the life, so that gradually the polluting sin is conquered and eventually eliminated. In this sense, man is cleansed and purified from his sins (for a while, at least), just as the dirty hands and clothes of a little boy are cleansed by water.

We return to the conversation between the Pharisee named Nicodemus and Jesus that took place under the cover of darkness. It is the encounter that results in John 3:16, surely the best-known verse in the Bible (especially at sporting events)! The centerpiece of that conversation was the Holy Spirit, and Jesus used two different symbolic illustrations for the Holy Spirit in that conversation, one of which was water. In verse 5, the Savior says, *"Truly, truly, I say to you, unless one is born of water and the Spirit, he cannot enter the kingdom of God."*

It is not easy to determine the actual meaning of the word water in this instance. It may be a direct symbol of the Spirit. On the other hand, it may be a symbol of baptism, which is by water and is both a sign and seal of the work of the Holy Spirit. In either case, water is closely associated with the Spirit. The bottom line is that Jesus says that in order to enter into the kingdom of heaven we must be born of the Spirit, who cleanses us from our sins just as water washes away dirt.

The same idea is found in Psalm 51—King David's most famous (but not only) psalm in which he publicly confesses his sinfulness. In that psalm, David prays (and we frequently repeat as our own prayers), *"[2]Wash me thoroughly from my iniquity, and cleanse me from my sin...[10]Create in me a clean heart, O God, and renew a right spirit within me......[11]take not your Holy Spirit from me"* (verses 2, 10-11). Ezekiel uses the same figure of speech when he writes; *"[25]I will sprinkle clean water on you, and you shall be clean from all your uncleanness, and from all your idols I will cleanse you...[26]a new spirit I will put within you"* (Ezekiel 36:25-26). The Apostle Paul makes a definite reference to the cleansing power of the Spirit through regeneration when, in writing to his young protégé Titus, says that God *"saved us...by the washing of regeneration and renewal of the Holy Spirit"* (Titus 3:5). The parallel use of water and the Spirit in these three passages illustrates symbolically to us the cleansing power of the regenerating and sanctifying Spirit.

Recall at the beginning of this discussion of water as a symbol of the Holy Spirit there were two different reasons the Bible uses this particular symbol. Water is not only useful to cleanse away dirt, but it is also necessary for life, whether that life is human, animal or plant. A good spring can bubble forth an abundance of water, so that even after buckets of water are drawn, the well is still overflowing. A spring on higher ground—as it spills over and downward—will cause greenness and life. In fact, it can turn a dead, barren desert into an oasis, or into the productive banks of the Nile River valley in Egypt or the lushness of southern California.

Using this easily observed fact, the Bible describes the Spirit and his influence. In John 7:37-39, Jesus said (actually the text says he *"cried out"*), *"[37]If anyone thirsts, let him come to me and drink. [38] Whoever believes in me, as the Scripture has said, "Out of his heart will flow rivers of living water" ' [39]Now this he said about the Spirit..."* What John is saying is that if someone is a Christian, the fruit of sanctification (that is, the evidence that spiritual growth is taking place in his or her life) will be like rivers of living water. This topic was covered at length in Chapter Ten on baptism and fullness.

Think about it this way. When a Christian does good works, even those works are a result of the grace of God as his Spirit flows from us like a river. Those rivers of good works have a source. That source is not us; the source is the Holy Spirit. Elsewhere Jesus put it this way. *"The water that I will give him will become in him a spring of water welling up to eternal life."* (John 4:14) When someone believes in Jesus, the Holy Sprit dwells in his life and causes him to desire to live a Christian life. The Spirit acts as a fountain within the Christian, from which these rivers of good works flow out to others. In this way, the Spirit continues to produce new life.

This is how water symbolically describes, in two different ways, the work of the Spirit—His cleansing and his life-giving power. We all should be asking ourselves if we know the Spirit of God as water. Are we being cleansed by him from our sinful habits, and is he really a fountain to our souls, causing us to bring forth those rivers of good works?

The second important biblical symbol for the Holy Spirit is *wind*. This is the second symbol that Jesus included in his conversation with Nicodemus. In John 3:8 he says, *"The wind blows where it wishes, and you hear its sound, but you do not know where it comes from or where it goes. So it is with everyone who is born of the Spirit."*

The symbolism is pretty clear. First of all, the way in which the Spirit works in regeneration is mysterious. It cannot be thoroughly understood. He and his operations are not visible to the human eye. And that's the way it is with wind. Our eyes can see the results of the wind, but we can't see the actual wind that causes the result.

Many of us have seen the results of hurricanes in recent years. Several times, they have been so severe, they even affected the area of mountains in southwestern Virginia where I have been living for the past 20 years. We are hundreds of miles inland from the Atlantic and even more from the Gulf of Mexico. Trees have been bent and uprooted. Roofs of houses were torn off. Power lines fell down and electricity was cut off sometimes for days or even weeks at a time. The results can be seen by all, but no one has ever seen the wind that caused them. It is invisible.

That's the way it is with the Holy Spirit, says Jesus. One can see the results of the Spirit's work— holiness, good works, powerful lives. But one can never see the Holy Spirit. He is just like the wind. Thus, during the historical event of the Pentecost celebration in Jerusalem following Jesus' ascension, Luke records in Acts 2:2 that *"suddenly there came from heaven a sound like a mighty rushing wind, and it filled the entire house where they were sitting."* This was incontrovertible evidence of the presence of the Holy Spirit.

Not only does the symbolism of wind speak to the *mysterious nature* of the work of the Holy Spirit, it also speaks to the *power* of his work. The hurricane illustration mentioned above applies here as well. It takes a tremendous amount of power to break up buildings and tear down trees and utility poles. Likewise, it takes a tremendous amount of power in the life of every Christian to be able to withstand the temptations to sin that come from the self, the devil and the world. It takes power in the life of a believer to bring about the radical inward changes needed for true repentance. It takes power in the life of a believer to withstand the external attacks that we face every day. No one has that power in and of himself. We must constantly be depending on the indwelling power of the Holy Spirit.

The third aspect of this illustration of wind is one most folks don't automatically think of but it is an important aspect. That is the issue of the sovereignty of God. Meteorologists can tell us a lot about wind. They can trace its path. They can measure its speed. They can make predictions about what it will do, sometimes even with a modicum of accuracy! However, one thing they can't do is control the wind. They can't grab hold of a tornado and move it away from a populous urban area. They can't direct the path of a hurricane to a deserted shoreline. The wind is absolutely sovereign. Jesus tells us in John 3:8, *"the wind blows where it wishes."* The Holy Spirit is equally sovereign. He saves whomever he wants to, when he wants to, and by the method of his own choosing. No manmade system or activity can control the work of the Holy Spirit in his regenerating or sanctifying work.

A third symbol the Bible uses for the Holy Spirit is *breath*. This is closely related to the symbol of the wind. In fact, both in Old Testament Hebrew and in New Testament Greek, the very same word in each language can be properly translated as wind, breath or spirit. So it is no surprise that breath is a frequent symbol in the Bible.

While breath shares the "mysterious" or "invisible" nature of wind, it has a special aspect of its own that is important to understand. That aspect is that breath is something inside of a person and has some relationship to life itself. There is an old time saying, referring to someone who has died, that he or she has "given up the ghost." This comes from the King James Version translation of the word for wind, breath and spirit as "ghost." It results in the archaic terminology for the Holy Spirit as the "Holy Ghost." Well, it is true, isn't it? When someone dies, he gives up his breath. He ceases to breathe.

So, the symbolic relationship to the Holy Spirit is quite evident. When the breath-spirit is present, there is spiritual life present. If the breath-spirit is not present, there is spiritual death. As we saw in an earlier chapter, the coming of the Holy Spirit into an individual's life is exactly identical with the beginning of their spiritual life, or to use the symbol we are discussing, with the beginning of their spiritual breathing.

In addition to the bringing of spiritual life, this symbolism of breath has several other uses in the Bible. In Genesis 2:7, it is used to speak of natural life itself. We are told there, *"then the LORD God formed the man of dust from the ground and breathed into his nostrils the breath of life, and the man became a living creature."* This clearly is speaking of giving life itself.

We find a very unique use of this symbol in John 20:22, where Jesus, speaking to his circle of disciples who are to become apostles, says, *"And when he had said this, he breathed on them and said to them, 'Receive the Holy Spirit.' "* This event is not the point of regeneration for these disciples, nor is it the general giving of the Spirit for sanctifying purposes, which was to occur at Pentecost. Rather this was a very special reception. These men were to serve in the apostolic office and were in need of special, even miraculous apostolic gifts. It was at this point they received those gifts.

There is yet a fourth use of the symbol of breath, and this is one to which we are all deeply indebted to the Spirit. For without it, we could never understand what we know about the Triune God and his work in the world. That is the aspect of inspiration of the Bible. In 2 Timothy 3:16, Paul tells us that, *"All Scripture is breathed out by God."* This term "breathed out" (or to use the older translation of this verse, "God-breathed") is what it means for the Bible to be inspired. It's not enough to say that the Bible is "made" or "created" by God. The Scriptures are more than a created entity, more than a "thing." The Scriptures are alive. They are referred to as the "word of life." This act of breathing brings them to life through the inspiration to men whom God chose to become the authors.

There are several other symbols for the Holy Spirit in the Bible, including *fire, oil,* and a *dove.* We will cover each of these just briefly. Everyone understands fire. Fire is power. It can consume everything it touches. Figuratively speaking, people are spoken of as being on fire, meaning that they are powerfully aroused and ready to consume things around them for their purpose.

Luke tells us in Acts 2:3 that the coming of the Holy Spirit at Pentecost was not only characterized by the sound of rushing wind, but tongues *"as of fire"* also appeared. We understand this symbolized not only the new power that believers in Jesus had received, but also their own arousal to fulfill the promise that Jesus had made just prior to his ascension. In Acts 1:8 he said, *"...you will receive power when the Holy Spirit has come upon you, and you will be my witnesses in Jerusalem and in all Judea and Samaria, and to the end of the earth."*

Oil is a symbol derived from several Old Testament passages. Back in those days, it was the practice to anoint the prophets, priests and kings by pouring oil on their heads. This anointing symbolized their appointment to the office and the giving of the Spirit to qualify and gift them for their work. Therefore, oil was a symbol of the Spirit of God.

Finally, all four of the gospel writers tell us that the descending of the Holy Spirit upon Jesus at his baptism was *"as a dove."* The Bible, however, does not tell us why this symbol is used to give a greater insight into the many aspects of the work of the Holy Spirit. Doves are generally understood today as symbols of peace. While Jesus was meek and mild, and did indeed bring us peace (His special peace that surpasses all understanding), we must not limit our understanding of the Holy Spirit's settling upon him peacefully as a dove to be the whole significance of the symbol. Jesus was far more than simply a peacemaker!

In conclusion, we should all stand amazed at how helpful the Bible is at giving us symbols by which we can better understand the person and work of the Holy Spirit. As the third person of the Trinity, the Holy Spirit deserves our understanding. If we want to know how to repent of our sins and grow spiritually (as we should), to understand God's mysterious work in our lives and come to grips with God's sovereignty in all things related to our salvation, then we must thank God for these amazing symbols of the Holy Spirit. We must appreciate that he allows us to know him more and more each day through his help in understanding these images. And we must praise him for the work of his Spirit in our lives, bringing us to salvation, and helping us to live lives worthy of his residence within us.

Appendices

Appendix A
List of Charismatic Gifts

#	Verse	NIV	ESV	Notes
1 Corinthians 12				
1	8	Wisdom	Wisdom	
2	8	Knowledge	Knowledge	
3	9	Faith	Faith	
4	9	Healing	Healing	
5	10	Miracles	Miracles	
6	10	Prophecy	Prophecy	
7	10	Distinguish between spirits	Distinguish between spirits	
8	10	Speaking in tongues	Various kinds of tongues	
9	10	Interpretation of tongues	Interpretation of tongues	
10	28	Apostles	Apostles	
11	28	Prophets	Prophets	
	28	Teachers	Teachers	Same as 2
	28	Workers of miracles	Miracles	Same as 5
	28	Healing	Healing	Same as 4
12	28	Helps	Helping	
13	28	Administration	Administrating	
	28	Speaking in tongues	Various kinds of tongues	Same as 8
	30	Interpret	Interpret	Same as 9
Romans 12				
	6	Prophecy	Prophecy	Same as 6
14	7	Service	Service	
	7	Teaching	Teaching	Same as 2
15	8	Encouraging	Exhorting	
16	8	Giving	Contributing	
17	8	Leadership	Leading	
18	8	Showing mercy	Doing acts of mercy	

#	Verse	NIV	ESV	Notes
Ephesians 4				
	11	Apostles	Apostles	Same as 10
	11	Prophets	Prophets	Same as 6
19	11	Evangelists	Evangelists	
20	11	Pastor-teachers	Pastor-teachers	
1 Peter 4				
21	9	Hospitality	Hospitality	
	10	Administration	Stewards	Same as 11
	10	Speaks (preaches)	Speaks	Same as 20
	11	Serves	Serves	Same as 15

Appendix B
Speaking in Tongues Today

Many Christians today believe that the Holy Spirit does indeed continue to give the miraculous gift of "speaking In tongues"—while the historical Presbyterian position says that such gifts have ceased. What are the issues to be considered in examining this issue?

I. Biblical considerations

   A. Mark 16:17-18 is the only place in the gospels where speaking in tongues is mentioned. *"And these signs will accompany those who believe: in my name they will cast out demons; they will speak in new tongues; ¹⁸they will pick up serpents with their hands; and if they drink any deadly poison, it will not hurt them; they will lay their hands on the sick, and they will recover."*

      1. Nearly all biblical scholars agree that there are three sections of the Bible that are almost certainly not part of the original "autographs" but were later, uninspired additions: 1 John 5:7 (explicit mention of the Trinity), John 7:53—8:11 (story of the woman charged with adultery) and Mark 16:9-20 (known as the long ending of Mark).

      2. The passage in Mark speaks not just of tongues, but also of snake handling and drinking poison. It is most improbable that one would be valid today and not the other two.

      3. This passage does not add anything significant to biblical truth.

B. Acts 2:4-11 is the earliest record of Christians speaking in tongues. *"And they were all filled with the Holy Spirit and began to speak in other tongues as the Spirit gave them utterance. [5]Now there were dwelling in Jerusalem Jews, devout men from every nation under heaven. [6]And at this sound the multitude came together, and they were bewildered, because each one was hearing them speak in his own language. [7]And they were amazed and astonished, saying, 'Are not all these who are speaking Galileans? [8]And how is it that we hear, each of us in his own native language? [9]Parthians and Medes and Elamites and residents of Mesopotamia, Judea and Cappadocia, Pontus and Asia, [10]Phrygia and Pamphylia, Egypt and the parts of Libya belonging to Cyrene, and visitors from Rome, [11]both Jews and proselytes, Cretans and Arabians—we hear them telling in our own tongues the mighty works of God.'"*

1. These were clearly foreign languages (at least 12 different language groups were present). They were understood *without* interpreters.

2. Salvation came through truth of the gospel, not the language spoken.

3. This is the only occurrence in the Bible in which non-Christians heard [and understood] the tongues spoken.

C. Acts 10:45-47 reads, *"And the believers from among the circumcised who had come with Peter were amazed, because the gift of the Holy Spirit was poured out even on the Gentiles. [46]For they were hearing them speaking in tongues and extolling God. Then Peter declared, [47]'Can anyone withhold water for baptizing these people, who have received the Holy Spirit just as we have?'"*

1. These were also foreign languages (not ecstatic utterances). (Obviously, the people were hearing foreign languages.)

2. Peter confirms the similarity to the original event in Acts 2.

D. Speaking in tongues was not at all an issue in the early Church until it came to the congregation at Corinth, which ended up with major problems concerning charismatic gifts. Paul took three chapters of a letter to straighten them out.

1. 1 Corinthians 12 and 13

a) 12:1-3 stresses that the primary evidence of the presence of the Holy Spirit in an individual's life is to confess that Jesus is Lord. It does not matter how we are "moved" to say it; what is important is that we say it.

b) 12:4-11 and 14-26 stress that the Holy Spirit gives different gifts to each believer and each believer is to use them for the common good of the Church.

c) 12:12-13 stresses a unity of one Spirit. (If speaking in tongues was a sign of the presence of the Holy Spirit, then *every* Christian would have the gift, but Paul says different people get different gifts.)

d) 12:27-30 stresses a diversity of gifts among believers. Again, no one gift is for all believers.

e) 13:1-7 stresses the difference between gifts of the Spirit and the fruit of the Spirit.

(1) The "love" chapter cannot be separated from the chapters on charismatic gifts.

(2) Paul says it is the fruit of the Spirit that is evidence of the Spirit's presence in the life of a Christian, not tongues.

f) 13:8-13 stresses when gifts will end.

(1) All gifts will end someday.

(2) Gifts related to the giving of revelation are no longer needed.

2. 1 Corinthians 14 teaches specifically about the nature and purpose of tongues.

a) Verses 1-5 indicate that gifts must always be used for others, not for self.

b) Verses 6-13 say prophecy is superior to tongues.

(1) Paul had the gift of tongues, but wouldn't use it.

(2) Tongues are likened to bad music.

c) To paraphrase verses 14-15, *"I will pray in church with my understanding in a language which every worshipper can understand. When I do this, I will still be praying with my spirit (the spirit which would be exclusively active if I prayed only in tongues), but I will be praying also with my understanding."*

d) The importance of verse 18 is significant. (Most Pentecostals say this is proof of the value of speaking in tongues)

(1) In the Apostolic age, the gift had value (to authenticate the Bible).

              (2) Paul says there is only a limited value of the gift that he has and others don't have.

      e) Verse 19 states that worship involves understanding, therefore tongues are a hindrance to worship.

      f) Verses 20-25 repeat the value of prophesy over tongues.

              (1) Tongues used in Old Testament didn't help Israel.

              (2) Non-Christians will think people who speak in tongues are a little wacky.

              (3) Prophecy is better.

      g) Verses 26-33 give directives for public worship, when speaking in tongues is practiced in the Corinth church.

              (1) A limited number should speak.

              (2) Only one at a time speaks.

              (3) There *must* be an interpreter present.

              (4) Tongues are forbidden with the wrong motive; they cause confusion.

   3. Summary: Just because tongues were practiced in New Testament churches does not necessarily mean they are valid in the Church today.

II. What about the practice of speaking in tongues in private?

   A. There is no longer any purpose for speaking in tongues.

   B. Scripture discourages private tongues (1 Cor 14:13).

C. Christians are supposed to use their spiritual gifts to encourage and build up others—private tongue speaking can't do that.

D. Spiritual gifts are service gifts and therefore given by God for ministry to others.

III. The Presbyterian Church in America, at their initial General Assembly, appointed a study committee to deal with the issue of miraculous gifts. So important was this issue in the last part of the 20th Century that this new Church made this the topic of their very first study committee. The final report in the form of a Pastoral Letter was adopted in September 1974 at the Second General Assembly, and has been a frequently cited position in guiding the presbyteries of the Church to make decisions as to acceptable candidates for licensure and ordination. As a Pastoral Letter, the PCA position on tongues is somewhat of a compromise. Here are the essential points.

A. Officers cannot hold to any view that connects tongues to new revelation.

B. Churches must not allow the practice of tongues in worship if it in any way results in confusion or disunity (which happens frequently).

C. The practice of speaking in tongues in private should not exclude an individual from membership.

See the PCA Historical Center website for the full text: www.pcanet.org/history/documents/pastoralletter.html.

The body of Christ suffered a great loss in the death of the Rev. Dr. Edwin H. Palmer several years ago. The Christian community at large and the Christian Reformed Church in particular, have lost both a competent scholar and a dedicated servant of Christ.

Born on June 29, 1922, Ed Palmer grew up and went to school in Quincy, Massachusetts. He graduated from Harvard College (A.B.) in 1944, following which he served as first lieutenant in the U.S. Marine Corps 1943–1946. In 1949, he received his Th.B. degree from Westminster Theological Seminary and furthered his education at The Free University of Amsterdam, receiving his doctorate (Th.D.) there in 1953. His accomplishments and contributions were so respected by the Christian academic community that, in 1977, Houghton College conferred on him the honorary degree of Doctor of Divinity.

Dr. Palmer was a pastor, an educator, an author and a concerned citizen. He pastored Christian Reformed Churches in Spring Lake, Michigan (1953–1957); Ann Arbor, Michigan (1957–1960); and Grand Rapids, Michigan (1964–1968). He was the Instructor in Systematic Theology at Westminster Theological Seminary (1960–1964). He wrote numerous articles and pamphlets and two books, *The Five Points of Calvinism* and *The Holy Spirit.* Besides his being a frequent conference and convention speaker, Dr. Palmer served as National Chairman of the Board of Citizens for Educational Freedom (1964–1968) and Chairman of the New Jersey Right-to-Life Committee (1969–1972).

Rarely has the Church been privileged to experience the gifts of God exhibited in one man as they were in Ed Palmer, whose two overriding attributes were his dedication and selflessness. He was constantly consumed by the call of God—a call he always put ahead of personal ambition. That was most evident in his selfless dedication to supervising the translation of the Bible into the recently published New International Version (NIV).

Ed served as Executive Secretary for the Committee on Bible Translation for the NIV from 1968 until his death. In 1979, he was appointed General Editor of the proposed NIV Study Bible. He was unshakably committed to his part in seeing that the body of Christ had the best translation of Scriptures available, by which the reader could know the word of God with complete confidence and in his own idiom.

In every task Edwin Palmer undertook, he gave his best effort "as unto the Lord." His untimely death on September 16, 1980, has left those of us who knew him with many unanswered questions and unfulfilled hopes, but he left this life with a clear knowledge that he had served his Lord in total faithfulness.

Rev. Paul Zylstra aptly summed up Dr. Palmer's life in his meditation at the memorial service on September 19, 1980, at the Midland Park Christian Reformed Church, Midland Park, New Jersey, when he quoted from 2 Timothy 4:7,8 (NIV): Ed had "fought the good fight, ... finished the race, ... kept the faith. Now there is in store for [him] the crown of righteousness, which the Lord, the righteous Judge, will award to [him] on that day...." Ed now knows the joy of his reward. His contribution to the Church serves as the most fitting memorial to his life—a memorial the Church will cherish for generations to come.

N. David Hill

Scripture Index

Luke

1:15	124
1:35	6
11	109
11:1-4	108
2:40	42
3:21-22	43
4:1	40
4:1-14	38
4:8	47
4:14	41
4:18-19	44

John

1:29	122
1:29-33	118,122
3	53
3:3	56
3:5	145
3:6	57
3:7	57
3:8	57
3:1-8	50
3:1-15	142
3:16	21,145
3:2	56,61
3:3	63
3:5	57
3:8	148,150
4:14	147
7:37-39	125,126
	147
7:38	126
7:53—8:11	159
8:34	54
10:41	135
12:26	48
13:30-31	139
14:16	115
14:17	73
14:26	139

John (cont.)

15:5	70
15:15	139
15:26	8
16:7	8,12
17:19	78
17:21	70
20:21	139
20:22	152

Acts

1:8	153
1:16	31
1:26	93
10:45-47	160
13:52	125
16:7	4
2	161
2:2	149
2:3	153
2:4-11	160
4:8	125
4:31	125
6:2	48
9:17	125

Romans

1:18	18
1:20	28
3:10-12	19
6:14	71
7	67
7:15	67
8	73,113
8:26	113
8:27	113
8:38-39	101
8:1	101
8:7	54
8:9	73

Scripture Index

About the Author

Dr. Clements was ordained in July of 1974 in the National Presbyterian Church (the original name of the PCA). After several years as a pastor in Central Georgia Presbytery, he returned to the U.S. Navy, where he had previously spent 12 years on active duty prior to entering seminary. Having left as an enlisted man (Chief Petty Officer), he returned as a Navy Chaplain.

Serving ten additional years on active duty on assignments with Destroyer Squadrons in San Diego; at the Naval Air Station in Pensacola; as Chaplain for a nuclear-powered guided missile cruiser and a submarine tender in Norfolk, and finally as Chaplain of the Naval Hospital, Newport, RI, Don retired in 1985.

For the next 18 years, he pastored two "turn-around" church revitalizations of small churches in Blacksburg and Narrows, VA. On January 1, 2003 he moved full-time into a ministry he had developed called *Metokos Ministries— Encouragement for Small Churches.* Affiliated with the Presbyterian Evangelistic Fellowship (PEF) as an evangelist, Don works with small churches (mostly under 100 members) that need encouragement and resources to develop vision plans, go through pulpit transitions, and other specific needs. (Visit his website at *www.metokos.org.*)

Don holds an M.Div. (with honors) from Covenant Theological Seminary in St. Louis, and a D.Min. (in Adult Education) from Gordon Conwell Theological Seminary in South Hamilton, MA. He and his wife, Esther, live with their Cocker Spaniel "Shadow" in their newly remodeled retirement home in the Appalachian Mountain town of Narrows, Virginia, and they spend lots of time visiting their three grown daughters who currently live in Mississippi, South Dakota and Virginia.

www.ingramcontent.com/pod-product-compliance
Lightning Source LLC
Chambersburg PA
CBHW021101090426
42738CB00006B/447